The Baruntse Adventure

In the footsteps of Hillary across East Nepal

MARK HORRELL

"We were crossing a level corniced section just below a great cleft in the ridge, when Beaven ... thrust in his ice-axe ... A great fissure and a large section some 200 ft. long dropped away down the face ... We sat down further back, both considerably shaken and told one another of the very close shaves we had had."

George Lowe

THE BARUNTSE ADVENTURE

Footsteps on the Mountain Diaries

DAY 1
PLANES, LEGS AND AUTOMOBILES

Wednesday, 13 October 2010 – Num, Arun Valley, Nepal

I write this in a cool, terraced garden high up on a ridge overlooking the lush Arun Valley in eastern Nepal. Mark sits a few feet away from me outside a yellow mountain tent, tapping a message into his satellite phone. A lady's bra hangs on a washing line a metre in front of him, but that's incidental and I don't think he's noticed it yet.

We're back in the foothills of the Himalayas at the start of our expedition. My heart is glowing with anticipation for the weeks ahead. We have more than a month to trek west across passes and valleys, climbing 7,129m Baruntse on the way. The trail is remote, with very few villages, and we have an opportunity to see Everest from its rarely seen east side.

Getting here from Kathmandu has been a story in itself. It's involved one aircraft, four separate 4WD vehicles, a creaky wooden punt across a river, and

1

finally our feet; and now here we are at the village of Num in the Arun Valley.

We were supposed to fly to nearby Tumlingtar and walk from there, but Tumlingtar Airport has been closed for refurbishment. It was scheduled to re-open on Saturday, but this is Nepal; it still wasn't open by Monday, when we were due to fly, so we flew to Biratnagar on the Indian border and drove from there.

Three days of driving on winding dirt tracks through jungle foothills tested our stomachs as we lurched from side to side like a canoe on the ocean. I felt sorry for myself, until I realised that Dawa, our sirdar and climbing leader, was missing.

'Where's Dawa?' I said from the comfort of the front seat. Nine Nepalis were packed in behind me, but they insisted Mark and I travel in the front because – well, I guess we were paying the lion's share of the cost.

Our driver reached out of the window and tapped the top of his door.

'He jumped out of the window?' I joked. But the joke was on me.

'I think Dawa's on the roof,' Mark said.

'He's what – you're shitting me?'

But the next time we stopped, I got out and looked up behind me. There, squatting on a tiny piece of metal 2m by 3m, were a further six people squashed together like sardines. Dawa was grinning from ear to ear.

'How the hell do you manage to stay on?'

He didn't reply, but simply grinned more broadly as his rooftop companions laughed. I could only conclude that they must be glued there.

The road has recently been extended beyond Tumlingtar (though 'road' is a generous word for it). This has meant we've been able to catch up on our schedule and have lost no days. We bypassed the sprawling villages that extended endlessly beside the trail through the lower foothills, and arrived in the heart of mountain country.

Today's drive was something of an eye-opener too. It's amazing what terrain a Land Rover can cross – our driver relished the challenge, laughing whenever we reached a difficult bit, and cheering afterwards.

After Khandbari, the village where we stayed last night, the rutted mud track passed beyond the sprawl of villages and climbed switchbacks up a hillside blanketed with terraced rice fields. Here we came across a stricken tractor with one of its wheels removed. Our driver squeezed around with a bold and skilful piece of driving, but shortly afterwards a man in the back threw up. Then we had to release an old lady and her daughter because they couldn't take any more. They looked relieved as we pulled away. I'm guessing that rodeo wasn't one of the old lady's top skills.

How the people on the roof continued to stay put without falling off, I have no idea. As we wriggled in relative comfort, I sat in fear of somebody sliding down the windscreen onto the bonnet – a metaphorical two fingers thrust upwards at our cushy position in the front seat. There was a more comical moment when somebody's wallet flew off and landed in front of us. The driver screeched to a halt so that the owner could jump off and put the wallet back in his trouser pocket before it got tossed down the precipice to our left.

Eventually the track reached the top of a hillside and passed over a ridge. Here the mountain views opened out before us, and a white wall of snow appeared on the horizon.

'Makalu!' our driver said – the fifth highest mountain in the world.

We passed through the village of Chichila, where the names of several trekking lodges boasted a Makalu View. Dawa and I were not convinced.

'I think it is Mera Peak,' Dawa said.

'I'm sure it's Chamlang,' I replied.

Shortly before midday the road ended on a ridge beside a collection of tin shacks in rhododendron forest. Here our kitchen team of Sarki the cook and his assistants Pasang, Karma and Mingma were waiting for us. They ushered us into one of the shacks for fried chips and coleslaw.

Dawa was alarmed to discover that seven of the porters we were expecting had not appeared. Another trekking group had offered them more money at the last minute and they decided to desert. But extra hands were quickly rustled up, including a man who hitched a ride with us from Khandbari. He had intended to stop in Chichila, but now it looks like he's going to end up walking all the way to Lukla, many days' trek across the mountains. His wife will be furious.

We had only a short walk this afternoon, down the ridge to the village of Num. The trail started in darkness as it wound through rhododendron forest. But after half an hour it opened out to give fine views of steep forested hills across the green and pleasant Arun Valley.

Narrow trail and hut above the Arun valley

Our second guide – another Pasang – pointed out Num village, a few miles away on the lower end of the ridge. The path gently curled to the right and dropped towards it, past terraced fields and the occasional thatched bamboo house. The sun was out, but the climate is comfortable here at 1,500m altitude, with plenty of shade from the trees.

Shortly before reaching Num at 4pm, we were overtaken by a porter carrying a live pig in a basket behind him. The pig squealed 'hi' as they raced past.

Num is a relative metropolis. It was lively as we walked through, shops thrumming with busy trade, and fifty or so spectators cheering on a game of volleyball in the main village square. One team was kitted out neatly in identical red kit, but the rag-tag bunch of misfits wearing dirty jeans, old T-shirts and multi-coloured bandanas on their heads seemed to be having the better of the play.

Sarki chose a teahouse at the far side of the village, with a pleasant garden at the back for camping. As soon as we arrived, a dozen or so porters emerged from wherever they were hiding and deposited their loads. Pretty girls stood around on the back step of the teahouse, staring in curiosity at our disparate bunch.

'The porters will be pleased with this place,' I said to Mark.

Left to find their own rooms for the night they always choose the houses with the pretty girls, and this time they needed to go no further.

Later this evening we crowd into a cosy little room at the back of the house for dinner. It's sparsely furnished with a wooden table in the middle of the room for me and Mark, a large bench at one side for Sarki and his kitchen crew, and an open fire in one corner, where one of the girls cooks dinner for the rest of the family. It's smoky and dark; we have to read by the light of our head lamps.

I know Dawa comes from a village nearby called Hungdung (or Honggong, as it's named on the map). I ask him about his family and end up getting more than I bargained for.

He becomes very sad as he relates his tale.

'My mother die when I was four years old. I don't know exactly when I was born. My passport says I'm 32, but I think I'm 34, so she die 30 years ago. My father die in the spring this year in an accident. He try to climb tree but the branch break, and he fell and die. He was missing for two days, so the people of my village look for him in the forest and find his body.'

I am sorry that I asked, but perhaps he wanted to tell us after all. The story breaks my heart and I feel an affinity with him. My mother died in similar circumstances; many years ago now, she fell down a bank and drowned in a lake while she was out walking on the moors near her home. We are quiet for several minutes watching smoke rise from the fire and snake across the room.

Dawa leaves the house and later in the evening he returns with a grinning young porter.

'Do you recognise this man?' he asks.

Mark and I rack our brains, but we don't think we've seen him before.

'Was he with us in the Land Rover?' I ask tentatively.

Dawa and the porter look disappointed.

He turns out to be Pemba, one of the porters on our

Mera and Island Peak expedition last year.[1] The eight porters we hired for that expedition were the best, friendliest and most helpful I've ever had. I'm sorry I didn't recognise him, but I'm glad to see he's with us again.

'Is he the only one?' I ask.

'He not with us,' Dawa says. 'He came to say *namaste* [hello].'

Dawa explains that Pemba has retired from portering because he wants a regular wage, and portering jobs tend to be seasonal. It's the second time today that we've had signs of porter trouble. I go to sleep with misgivings. Are these porter difficulties going to become a theme that blights our expedition? I hope not.

---

1 See my book *Islands in the Snow*

DAY 2
HIMALAYAN WORKOUT

Thursday, 14 October 2010 – Seduwa, Arun Valley, Nepal

We wake at 6am to pack our bags and send our quickest porters on their way, so that they reach camp before us. After they're gone we have a leisurely breakfast.

Dawa is still trying to work through the porter issues. Porters are always slower getting ready on the first day of a trek as they argue over load sizes and who should carry what. This time we also have the question of how to transport the loads that were meant for our seven missing porters. Some emergency porters were found, but not seven. Four of the strongest porters agree to carry 45kg each – one and a half times the usual load – which solves the issue for today. Dawa hopes that we'll be able to recruit more porters as we pass through villages along the trail. They are generally paid by the kilo, so it's usually not difficult finding volunteers for extra load carrying. Sometimes porters will ask to carry more.

Mark and I leave with Pasang the guide (as opposed to Pasang the kitchen assistant) at 8am. We start the day's walk by dropping down, down, down through forest and past rice fields to the Arun River 800m below Num.

A narrow footbridge spans the river about 15m above the water. Mark slips on the damp rock steps leading up to it, falling on his backside and cutting the palms of his hands. I should be sympathetic, but I'm reminded of an incident in Kathmandu a few days ago, when the rickshaw we were travelling in accelerated over a speed bump, pitching Mark over the handlebars. We'd both been drinking. The driver turned around to apologise, and was surprised when I started roaring with laughter. He was even more surprised when Mark demonstrated the extent of his intoxication by handing over a hefty tip when we reached our hotel.

It's lucky that I'm walking behind Mark as we approach the bridge. He can't see the trouble I'm having trying not to laugh.

When we are on the other side of the river it's up, up, up again, this time on a south-facing hillside. At least the forest affords us some protection from the sun. At 10.30 we stop by a wooden shack beside the path. We spend two hours over lunch as Sarki and the crew spread their pots and dishes over the terrace and cook us a hot meal. I read my book, while Mark sleeps with a blue buff pushed over his face.

At 12.30 we resume our climb. Mark and Pasang

shoot off at a fair old rate; I sweat like a pig trying to keep up with them in the humid air. Since we're in no particular hurry I eventually decide to slow down. Every so often I have to stop and wipe the sweat from my sunglasses and eyes. Despite sweating buckets, the walking is easy, mainly up stone steps through the forest, occasionally breaking into the open as we pass through rice fields.

Descending through rice fields

Soon we're high above the river and looking back across the valley to Num. The village crests the ridge on the hillside behind us. The top half of the hill is split between forest and rice terraces, all the way down to about 500m below the village – here, the slope steepens to cliff faces and terrain too vertical to cultivate.

Small pockets of housing dapple the hillside, but there are not many, and the farmland surrounding them is substantial. I ask Pasang if the fields are owned by the village or by the individuals living in the houses further down the hill. He explains that while some may be privately owned, much of the land will be under common ownership.

We pass the first trekkers we have seen since arriving in Biratnagar: a lone Australian on his way up, and a French couple on their way down. The Australian is travelling with half a dozen porters, guides and kitchen crew, and the French couple ask him if he speaks any Nepali to communicate with them.

'Jeez, they asked me if I speak any Nepali,' he says as he passes us. 'I don't even speak any French.'

Mark and I glance at each other.

'Of course, it's debatable whether Australians can speak English,' Mark says.

We reach our campsite in the village of Seduwa at 3pm. The village has a number of trekking lodges, and most, including ours, have wide grass terraces for camping.

We started the morning at 1,500m in Num, and descended to 700m to cross the river before climbing all the way back up to 1,700m in Seduwa. This is a relatively low altitude for a trek in the Himalayas; despite overcast conditions, it's been on the warm side all day. The humidity of the lush rhododendron forest hasn't helped. By the time we arrive in camp we're both dripping with sweat.

Unlike Mark, I resist the temptation to take my shirt off and hang it on the line. The lodge owners have a young family of seven children ranging from toddlers to teenagers. They are younger than the girls at last night's lodge and Mark might have been more discrete. His chest is lined with inch-thick mats like a mountain gorilla's. These kids have probably been brought up hearing tales of the yeti, and Mark's appearance might frighten them. Fortunately, unlike the girls in last night's lodge, these kids don't seem at all inquisitive. They happily ignore him and carrying on playing.

I take out my diary, which causes Mark to grin.

'What's today's entry going to say?' he asks. 'Walked uphill. Sweated a lot.'

'You should keep a diary yourself,' I reply.

There's a balcony area on the upper storey of the lodge. We have tea and biscuits while looking out across the Arun Valley to Num on the ridge opposite. It's a picturesque setting with large wooded hills rising up beyond. We enjoy it briefly before the sun goes down at six o'clock. The balcony has a low roof and I keep cracking my head when I stand up.

Dawa joins us after dinner. He's reading a dictionary to try and improve his English, but I'm not sure this is the best way.

'We have tens of thousands of words nobody uses,' I say.

I illustrate this point when I open the dictionary at random.

'Humdinger, hurly-burly and hussy,' I read out.

I guess these words could prove useful if Dawa ever reads the opening scene of Macbeth.

DAY 3
INTO SHERPA COUNTRY

Friday, 15 October 2010 – Tashigaon, Makalu Barun, Nepal

I can't quite believe that last month I tried to climb the sixth highest mountain in the world. For four weeks I camped at 5,700m at the foot of Cho Oyu in Tibet. I had always been told that it was the easiest 8,000m peak in the world to climb, and from the Tibetan plateau it did indeed look like a gentle dome of snow (albeit an enormous one).

But appearances are deceptive. For two weeks the temperature was mild, but it snowed incessantly, piling up those gentle slopes with soft powder. Then the weather turned on its head. Suddenly it was very cold, but we experienced crisp, clear days of beautiful sunshine. This created a hard crust on top of the soft powder and the slopes became very dangerous. There were many avalanches. Some Sherpas were badly injured trying to fix ropes to the summit when they were catapulted hundreds of metres. We abandoned the expedition.

It's exactly two weeks since I left Cho Oyu Base Camp and the other side of the Himalayan divide. I couldn't be anywhere more different from the dry desert landscape of Tibet. It feels more like trekking through a jungle. This point is underlined when I start the morning by putting on the still-wet clothes that I trekked in yesterday.

Today's walk is a little cooler and easier than yesterday's, although it's still very warm. I have to keep finding excuses for not keeping up with the rapid pace that Pasang and Mark are setting at the front. Each time I stop for a photo I look up to find myself 50m further behind.

We continue to walk past rice fields dotted with isolated farmhouses, and I get chased by a small child demanding I take a photograph of her. Photographing small children doesn't carry the same stigma in Nepal as it does back home in the UK, where parental permission is required. I'm able to pass on without getting chased by an angry father.

A short while later I catch up with Mark and Pasang, who are waiting for me yet again.

'Sorry about that,' I say. 'That little girl back there insisted I take a photo.'

'Yeah, I heard that,' Mark replies. 'You didn't get arrested then?'

I tell him about an incident that happened three years ago when I walked the Tamang Heritage Trail north of Kathmandu.[2] I was trekking with our friend

---

2 See my book *Himalayan Diaries*

Siling, who owns a trekking agency called The Responsible Travellers (who also arranged the logistics for this trek).

Siling stopped to photograph some colourfully dressed children, who were happy to be snapped in their traditional clothing. But in some parts of Nepal, locals believe that taking photos of a person steals their soul and captures it in the camera. The children ran off to tell their mother they'd just had their pictures taken. She was furious with them, but it was a great photo. Siling is a devout Buddhist and he thought long and hard about the karmic significance of publishing the photo in his trekking brochure. I don't know if he consulted a lama or lit butter lamps at Swayambhunath, the Buddhist temple near to his home in Kathmandu, but he published the photo.

The trail contours around the hillside away from the Arun Valley, rising gently into mixed forest. We're now above the level of cultivated rice fields and into the land of Sherpas. Evidence of this appears in the form of small stupas and mani stones that have started appearing at intervals along the trail. Stupas are Buddhist monuments with a square base, a dome-shaped central portion and a spiked top section. They are supposed to be an abstract representation of the Buddha seated in meditation. They kind of look like elaborate headstones for somebody's grave, but they are not. Although the Buddha was said to have had his ashes divided and interred in various stupas around India, they are solid structures and they do not have anyone's remains buried beneath them.

Mani stones are rocks painted or inscribed with the Buddhist mantra *om mani padme hum*. Some are huge boulders left behind by a landslide; others are smaller stones assembled into a wall.

It's good luck to pass all of these monuments on the left-hand side, or else the prayers inscribed upon them will be read backwards by the deities. Although we are not superstitious, we don't want to upset Pasang by walking on the right. In any case, it has now become a habit for us. Even if passing a stupa or prayer wall clockwise involves a diversion from the main trail, we do it anyway.

We reach the rambling village of Tashigaon at 2,200m – a series of mud houses with woven bamboo roofs – which sprawls up a hillside in the forest. At 12.30 we reach a small trekking lodge at the very top of the village with a wide flat terrace looking all the way back down the route we've just trekked. This is our rest stop for the day, and a very pleasant spot it is, too.

Sitting on a bench on the lawn, Mark and I have tea and biscuits as we look across the folds of forested hillside towards the Arun Valley. Behind and above us the forests continue to rise for 1,000m over a brow. We have a long climb tomorrow – but for now we can relax.

Our swift pace today means that our porters are a long way behind us, so we take our time over lunch. Afterwards I lie down on the grass with my rucksack as a pillow and fall asleep. When I wake up half an hour later the first porters have arrived with our bags and someone has pitched our tent.

I will never tire of this Himalayan trekking lifestyle.

It's a little cooler now that we've climbed higher into the forest, but it feels like it's still going to be an evening for eating outside in relative comfort. In the end, we have dinner in a clean wood-panelled room at the end of the lodge, which is probably just as well. There seem to be a few insects about tonight, not to mention leeches – I had to pull one off my stomach earlier in the day.

DAY 4
PORTER TROUBLE

Saturday, 16 October 2010 – Khongma, Makalu Barun, Nepal

Our day starts with a porter issue and things goes downhill from there (metaphorically, not literally, as we have a 1,400m ascent ahead of us).

The kitchen crew wake us with bed tea shortly after dawn, at 6am. It's going to be a long day. We pack our duffle bags as soon as we vacate the tent. I notice the porters seem to be slower getting ready this morning. Normally they are standing over us as we load up, ready to take our bags, but this morning we finish our packing alone. I think nothing of it and go inside the teahouse for breakfast.

After I've eaten and I go back outside to brush my teeth, our kit bags are still sitting there on the lawn and Dawa is arguing with some of the porters. The discussion seems to be getting heated. Before long the scales are out, loads are dismantled, and the weighing begins. Porters leave the campsite one by one as loads are agreed, but at the end of the weighing procedure there are still half a dozen porters left, and a new debate seems to be raging.

I return to the breakfast table and continue reading, while Mark watches for a bit longer to try and figure out what's going on.

'Now some of them seem to be asking for bigger loads. They've totally shot themselves in the foot,' he murmurs, with a slightly contemptuous laugh.

Dawa comes in to explain what's happening. Porters are paid 1,000 rupees a day to carry a single load of 30kg. They have to carry their own personal kit on top of this. In some circumstances they can volunteer to carry extra weight, for which they're paid proportionately.

Porters who are prepared to carry one or two extra kilos also get their food paid for out of expedition funds. It can cost up to 500 rupees a day for the porters to feed themselves, so this is a perk that most of them choose to accept. And this is where the problem is now arising. By rigidly insisting their loads are measured at exactly 30kg, the half dozen porters remaining have suddenly realised they must pay for their own food. Now they're squabbling over how they can divide the remaining equipment so that each of them can take an extra one or two kilos.

In the end they're back to where they started, and we've wasted a good hour at the start of a long day.

'We pay them good money and feed them, but still they want more,' Dawa says.

Incidents like this don't do their chances of getting a decent tip any good either, but it's still early in the expedition and they have plenty of time to get back in our (and Dawa's) good books.

When Pasang, Mark and I leave shortly after 8.30, Dawa and the porters are still arguing over our personal kit bags, but we're keen to get going. We brace ourselves for a long wait for the bags after we reach camp this afternoon.

It doesn't take more than a few hours for me to forgive our porters for their recalcitrance. The weather is horrible and in the circumstances they end up doing a sterling job. There is a light drizzle when we leave camp which gets steadily heavier as we climb deeper into forest. We have to stop and put our waterproof jackets and rucksack rain covers on. But still some of the porters confound us with their stubbornness. They have all been issued with waterproof jackets and trousers in a matching brown colour, and they all carry good boots and shoes for the difficult terrain we are sure to encounter. Yet some of the porters are slow to put on their waterproofs and many still choose to climb in flip-flops.

The thick forest shelters us from the worst of the downpour, but at ten o'clock we emerge into a clearing and realise it's raining buckets. Sarki and the kitchen crew are sheltering underneath a small bamboo shack where a cow herder has lit a fire. We pile in with them. One by one the porters stop and warm themselves for a short while before moving on.

After half an hour the rain has died down a little, so Pasang, Mark and I continue walking. Ten minutes later, we come to a huge natural cave underneath an overhanging rock face. It's dry underneath, and although it's only 10.30, Sarki has decided it's likely to be the only suitable place to unpack their things and cook lunch. We stay for an hour and a half, which gives Dawa and the porter stragglers time to move past us.

The rest of the afternoon passes monotonously but with speed as we make good time up through the forest. Mark and I are both acclimatised from previous expeditions. He climbed Stok Kangri, a 6,000m peak in India, while I reached 7,150m on Cho Oyu in Tibet. This means that Pasang can lead us up the 1,400m of today's climb at a fast pace, instead of taking it easy to let us acclimatise.

It takes just 40 minutes to climb 350m up a rocky path through forest until we reach another bamboo shack where we can shelter for a few minutes. Then we climb more or less continuously through forest for another hour and a half.

Finally we crest a rise at an altitude of 3,600m, where the forest thins, and we come across some mani walls. A few minutes later we reach a teahouse with landscaped grass terraces for camping. It's three o'clock and still raining heavily, so we decide to use the simple dormitory upstairs rather than putting up tents in a garden that has become a quagmire.

I'm soaking wet from the rain, but have also been sweating buckets. I exchange my base layer for a fleece and shiver for a bit while we wait for the duffle bags containing our dry clothes. It's a relief when the relevant porter arrives only about an hour later. Our wet things are hanging up all over the dorm and it's still cold. I'm confident they'll still be soaking wet tomorrow morning.

We are served dinner in the dorm, brooding over the gloomy prospects of better weather tomorrow.

DAY 5
'THE WETTEST TREK I'VE BEEN ON'

Sunday, 17 October 2010 – Mumbuk, Makalu Barun, Nepal

If anything, today is even worse. We start with a 6am wake-up, and I put on my soaking-wet gear – which has been hanging up all over the dorm without getting any drier. Now my clothes are freezing cold as well as damp. It's not a good start to the day.

At least it's not raining when we start trekking at 8am, but this doesn't last for long. Although the skies are relatively clear to begin with, we can see sheets of cloud hanging over the warmer forested hills far below us.

We climb beyond the tree line into a green carpet of dwarf rhododendron. About 40 minutes after starting out we reach the first pass, the Khongma La, at a little over 3,800m. There's a prayer wall at the top and we stop for a short rest. It's to be our only substantial rest until we reach camp three and a half hours later. This is because soon afterwards we climb higher up a ridge into cloud and the heavy rain begins.

We climb for another 200m through rhododendron thickets and reach another pass, the Keke La, at a little over 4,000m. Pasang doesn't pause here, but strikes onwards at a pace I don't try to keep up with. The path drops a little below the ridge and becomes increasingly rocky before climbing up to Shipton's Pass at 4,250m. The great mountain explorer Eric Shipton crossed here in 1952 after completing his second Everest reconnaissance from the Nepal side. I would like to have known what he saw, but there is not much hope of that – today we can see absolutely bugger all.

It was on this expedition that a curious incident occurred which, had it turned out differently, would have had a significant bearing on the annals of mountaineering history. Bored with walking, the New Zealanders George Lowe and Edmund Hillary came up with the marvellous idea of lashing their air mattresses together with sticks, and making a crude raft to sail down the Arun River. Shipton was walking a little ahead of them, and noticed they were in danger of being smashed to pieces by a large rock jutting out into the river. Beyond the rock was a sizeable whirlpool which they were heading directly towards. Shipton described what followed in his book *That Untravelled World*.

> *For a long and desperate moment I waited to see their raft smashed to pieces, 200 feet below me, against the very cliff I was standing on. Unable to do anything*

to avert the disaster, I could only wait and visualise
the collision and the struggling form of my friends
being hurled into the curling wave. Once in the
water they would be sucked under immediately.

After watching the two men whizz around the whirlpool a few times without getting thrown against the cliff, Shipton was eventually able to fish them out with a rope.

The following year Hillary became world famous when he made the first ascent of Everest with Tenzing Norgay. Lowe became rather less famous for being the man on the receiving end of Hillary's immortal words when he returned to the South Col.

'Well, George, we knocked the bastard off.'

Meanwhile, I have trouble keeping up with Pasang and Mark, and reach Shipton's Pass out of breath. They are waiting for me, but Pasang strikes on again as soon as I arrive. I have to call him back so that I can stop for five minutes and get my breath back.

'I thought you were supposed to be acclimatised,' Mark says with a snort.

'I am, but I can't keep going without stopping.'

A bigger problem is that I'm now quite cold. The remorseless rain has meant that I haven't warmed up since putting on my cold, wet gear this morning. I have a fleece in my bag, but I don't want to put it on. It's the only dry item I'm carrying, and I know I may have to wait for my dry clothes again after we reach camp.

Pasang and Mark stride ahead, but I have no intention of trying to keep up with them. I want to maintain a pace that keeps me warm without making me sweat. I don't want to arrive in camp too far ahead of the porters because I'll only get cold waiting for them. And to cap it all, we descend slippery wet rocks. There's just no point in rushing. I'm a slow ambler anyway, and I prefer not to race.

We descend a couple of hundred metres before climbing up to the final pass of the day, the Tutu La.

'Is this pass named after Archbishop Desmond Tutu?' I say to Mark as we cower behind a large rock at the top.

But Mark isn't in the mood for inane banter as the rain whips past and the rock offers poor shelter.

'I think this is the wettest trek I've been on,' he says.

This surprises me. He's completed more treks than I have, and although it's certainly wet, I can think of at least three that have been much worse: in the Rwenzoris in Uganda in 2006, in Nepal during the monsoon in 2007, and last year in Bhutan.

The Rwenzori Mountains in East Africa wouldn't be everyone's cup of tea, but I thoroughly enjoyed them in a weird kind of way. The mountains were carpeted in cloud forest, and the trails were a soggy paste of thick mud. Parts of the route were underwater; crossing these sections involved bog-hopping from tuft of grass to tuft of grass, or tightrope-walking along branches which had been laid across the path to keep hikers from sinking. I wore gaiters over my leather hiking boots, and Gore-Tex trousers over everything. Each evening my legs were caked in mud up to my thighs. I hung my waterproof trousers from the rafters of mountain huts to dry overnight, then put them on again the next morning. Most of our local guides wore wellies.

In 2007, I hiked Nepal's Tamang Heritage Trail in early June. The monsoon was expected any day; it finally hit me with buckets of fresh water on the last two days of the trek, as I returned through the Helambu region to Kathmandu. My trousers became so waterlogged that they kept slipping down as I walked. Then there was Bhutan, the tiny Himalayan kingdom a short distance to the east. Generally speaking, the further east you go in the Himalayas, the wetter it gets. When I walked the Snowman Trek, Bhutan's best-known long-distance trail, I never got to see 7,326m Chomolhari, one of the country's most beautiful mountains, because it was in cloud for days on end. On the last day, it rained so heavily that I could have filled a small lake from what I wrung out of my clothes. I waded along trails that had been converted into streams, and much of my gear was still wet when I returned home.

I don't agree with Mark, but there is still time for this trek to eclipse them all.

Beneath the final pass we descend 300m on a path that resembles a river tumbling over rocks. We have to take great care as we descend.

Camp is a dark stone hut at 3,800m, with a small shop, a fire, and five rudimentary beds at one end. I warm my hands on a mug of black tea before taking my upper layers off and putting on just a single dry fleece over my bare chest. To keep my wet clothes on underneath would only make me colder.

We reach the hut at 1pm, and it gradually becomes more crowded as porters arrive: ours, plus those of a Czech couple and the lone Australian we met a few days ago. The Czech couple intend to sleep in the hut. It's going to be very cosy in there – not to mention a bit grim – so we decide to camp.

By three o'clock the tents are up, our bags have arrived, we've eaten lunch, and I'm able to put on dry clothes and settle into a warm sleeping bag. My trekking gear is going to remain wet; I'm not looking forward to putting it on again tomorrow.

There's no sign of the weather getting any better. For the next five hours, the rain continues to hammer on the roof of the tent. To compound our discomfort, water begins to seep through at four of the corners. We trace the leak to some loops of material for hanging up equipment – the seams where the loops have been sewn are allowing the water to get through. We seal them up with duct tape to minimise the leakage onto our sleeping bags.

Mark manages to get a weather forecast on his satellite phone. We don't know how accurate it is, but rain is predicted above 3,500m until Thursday 21st. This would mean four more miserable days before anything can get dry. It also means Baruntse is getting loaded with snow and will be prone to avalanche.

Our mood is gloomy. I'm not having much luck

with weather in the Himalayas this year.

DAY 6
A CHANGE IN THE WEATHER

Monday, 18 October 2010 – Yangri Kharka, Barun Valley,
Nepal

We have a pleasant surprise this morning: the dark and dismal little hole we camped in yesterday has been transformed. For the first time since we arrived in camp, rain is no longer hammering on the roof, and when I look out of the front of the tent, I see blue sky.

We are camped in a natural bowl above a deep valley surrounded by rocky peaklets. A sea of lush dwarf rhododendron washes over everything around us, and small waterfalls cascade down the slopes above on their way to the campsite. A jagged snow peak rises up on the other side of the valley. High overhead, two layers of cloud appear to be moving in opposite directions – the wind is obviously brisk up there. Whether this clear weather will last is an open question, but it's nice to have a view after 48 hours of solid, heavy rain.

We're now on the same schedule as three other

trekkers – a lone Australian and a young Czech couple – and although the Aussie packs up and leaves camp early, the Czechs depart at more or less the same time as us, and we keep passing them throughout the day. We're impressed with their fitness. Mark and I are acclimatised and quick, but neither of us is carrying a large rucksack like he is, and she's no slouch either.

The trail drops steeply for 600m through rhododendron forest to the Barun River valley, on a rough path that demands attention. At the foot of the valley the Barun River flows steeply across our path in a torrent of icy rapids that have cut great banks of gravel through the forest. We turn left up the valley and follow it for the remainder of the day. There is a clear path to begin with, but every now and again, side streams and boulder fields trespass across it; the terrain becomes difficult as we boulder-hop across to regain the trail. We pause from time to time for short rests, leapfrogging the Czech couple in the process.

We pass several trekkers returning from Makalu Base Camp. One of them stops to talk to us.

'There was snow most days at base camp, and too much cloud and mist to get much of a view, but still there were moments you remember,' he says.

He seems wistful. After he has passed, I glance at Mark, who puts into words what I had been thinking.

'It sounds like he's had a shit trek.'

It also sounds like the rain and snow have been continuing for longer than three days, which means we may yet be arriving at Baruntse at just the right time.

An eerie cloud wafts up the Barun Valley and veils the forested slopes to either side like a gossamer shawl. It morphs into a light drizzle as we climb, and then light rain. The path gets muddier as the valley widens. We pass in and out of forest and through grassy meadows, crossing many side streams that have become swollen with water. We need good balance on the submerged stepping stones.

Sarki and Dawa debate whether to stop for lunch, but as the rain becomes heavier we decide to press on. We pass a crowd of porters huddled by the side of the path. One of them has found two kestrels fighting and picked them up. As he holds them by the wings, one in each hand, they continue to rake each other with their talons. When Dawa arrives, he persuades the porter to release them, but the kestrels have done so much damage to each other that they can no longer fly. Dawa casts one of them into the air, but it flaps uselessly before coming to rest in a tussock a few feet away. It sits like a brooding hen and makes no effort to move when anyone approaches. It's difficult to know how many injuries they sustained before the porter picked them up, but I'm sure his intervention didn't help.

We reach camp at Yangri Kharka at 12.30. Prayer flags adorn three stone huts in a wide meadow beside the river. We are flanked by pine forests that rise up the hillsides either side of us. The mist continues to drift eerily above the river, and the grass is waterlogged, but on another day this would be a pleasant camping spot.

The Czech couple go into one of the further stone huts while Mark and I troop up a wooden stepladder in the near one to inspect the accommodation. A large dormitory contains about a dozen hard beds. The roof is low and the room is dark, but it's dry, and we decide it's preferable to a tent – providing it doesn't get swamped with trekkers descending from Makalu Base Camp. We decide this is unlikely, and settle in.

Today we both took the precaution of carrying dry clothes in our day packs – including down jackets and fleece trousers – so we are warm within minutes, and don't have to shiver as we wait for the porters to arrive. It's been a short day, and a relatively dry one compared with the last two. This has been a blessed relief.

DAY 7
WEIRD LUNCHES

Tuesday, 19 October 2010 – Yak Kharka, Barun Valley, Nepal

This morning is even better. Dare we hope that Mark's weather forecast is wrong?

We have a relatively late start, bed tea at 7am; outside the teahouse the skies are blue. By 7.30 sunshine floods the grassy meadow of Yangri Kharka, and I have to put on sun cream for the first time in days. But while we might appreciate the change in the weather, my camera doesn't agree. Condensation forms on the inside of the lens, and I'm unable to clean it without taking the whole thing apart. For the first hour of the day, as I wait for the condensation to evaporate, I wander along frustrated: all this beautiful scenery and not one snap to remind me of it.

During his 1952 reconnaissance expedition, one of Eric Shipton's senior Sherpas, Dawa Tenzing, told a story of the Barun Valley. It was his first time in the valley, but Sherpa legend told of its existence. The valley was supposed to contain an invisible village,

Shangri-La, that was said to be a place of great beauty. It was home to gods and a place where holy men came to die. They asked Dawa Tenzing if he hoped to see the village as they descended the valley, but he replied wistfully that he had been too great a sinner.

We're not saints either, but perhaps we will see the village today. It certainly feels like somewhere magical as we set off up the Barun Valley at 8.30. More pleasant walking can scarcely be imagined – we amble in and out of pine woodlands and thickets of dwarf rhododendron, with spectacular cliff faces crowned with snow caps rising either side of us. Once or twice we sit down among rocks and relax for 20 minutes, taking in the breathtaking vistas that have been hidden from us for so long.

Porters take a rest in the Barun Valley

'This is more like it. This is what we came here for,' I say to Mark during one rest break.

'And there's currently no sign of it shitting up any time soon,' he replies in the direct manner that I'm accustomed to.

I'm not confident of the fine weather remaining all day, but I'm grateful for what we are granted.

After two hours we rise above the forest into open moorland. The valley is wide but remains hemmed in on both sides by vast cliffs. We reach another campsite among the rhododendrons, where a goat herder and his tiny daughter have stopped with their herd. Beyond us, the valley rises steeply to a plateau a few hundred metres above.

We wander slowly beside the river, and at 12.30 we pause at a hut just beneath the plateau. Pasang asks if we want to stop here for the day, or continue for half an hour to another *kharka* (meadow) on the plateau.

'What's best for the porters?' Mark asks.

'Sarki thinks here best,' Pasang replies.

'Then whatever Sarki wants to do, we do,' Mark says with a nod.

To me the day feels incomplete without reaching the top of the hill, and where we've stopped doesn't seem flat enough to camp, but I don't object – Mark is better than me at going with the flow. What's best for the porters may not be what's best for us, but sometimes it's good for me to take a lesson in acceptance from Mark. In any case, mist is rising up from lower down the valley. It looks like the good weather is over for the day.

We find the flattest pitch and help Pasang to erect our tent. These shorter days seem to be the best way to proceed until the weather improves.

An hour later we have lunch in the upstairs room of the hut. I sometimes find Sarki's cooking a bit weird, and today is a classic example: tinned baby corn on the cob, boiled green beans, tinned sausages, a hunk of cheese, and some sort of pancakey thing best described as a fried noodle hash brown. Five items sitting on a plate that go together like morris dancers in a mosh pit.

I wonder where these recipes come from. It isn't something you'd ever cook for yourself, but it's not a typical Nepali dish either. I suspect Sarki is trying too hard to vary the food from meal to meal because he believes this is what westerners prefer. But it just ends up bizarre. He makes some excellent normal food, which I'd be very happy to eat meal after meal: fried rice, noodles, pakora, *momos*, *dal bhat*. Last night, after I'd barely touched my lunch, he even treated us to pizza.

I'd like to steer him in the right direction, but with our limited capacity to communicate in a common language, I'm not sure how to do this without giving offence. It doesn't help that Mark happily wolfs down whatever is put in front of him and then sends his compliments to the chef. Sarki could serve us grilled cowpat and Mark would eat it. I'm definitely going to lose weight on this expedition.

At dinner, Dawa, a Buddhist, explains why the weather has been so bad this October in what is usually Nepal's prime trekking season.

'There are two Hindu festivals this month when people traditionally kill goat.'

The two-week festival of Dashain began just before our expedition started, and it may be one of the reasons why we've had difficulty obtaining porters. People return home from the city or from abroad to visit their families in villages all over the country. The festival celebrates the victory of the goddess Durga over a demon who had been terrorising the earth. Their battle lasted for nine days, and the first nine days of the festival symbolise this fight. While the Buddhist diet is predominantly vegetarian, the Hindu festival of Dashain is very much a celebration for meat eaters. It traditionally begins with the ritual slaughtering of a goat, but buffaloes, ducks, chickens and sheep are also offered up as sacrifices to Durga.

No sooner is Dashain over than Deepawali begins. Also known as Diwali, Tihar, or the 'Festival of Lights', this festival only lasts for five days, and seems to involve the worshipping of cows, dogs and crows.

I witnessed the start of Dashain four years ago when I trekked the Annapurna Circuit with some friends. As we passed through the village of Tukuche in the Kali Gandaki Valley, we could see a group of villagers wrestling with a goat on the trail ahead of us.

'I think this goat's going to get it,' my friend Huw said.

He had noticed that one of the men was brandishing a machete. Or perhaps it was the Gurkha weapon known as a kukri; I didn't have time to study it closely. The important fact was that it had a very big blade. This man was standing at the front end of the goat while two other men held its head. The rest of the crowd were tugging on the goat's body so that the poor thing's neck was stretched to optimum length. Huw had registered these details more quickly than I had. We were little more than 10m away and approaching fast when the executioner raised his enormous chopper and brought it down so firmly on the animal's neck that its head and body parted company.

It all happened so quickly that we walked past them in stunned silence, as if nothing unusual had happened. We were 20m beyond before any of us had collected our thoughts sufficiently to say something. I think it was Huw who spoke first.

'Fucking hell.'

'Yeah,' I replied.

There wasn't much more that any of us could say.

Our conversation with Dawa is having a similar effect on me. He is talking a strange jumble of sentences that don't seem to add up to anything. But Mark has put them all together more quickly and can see what Dawa is trying to say.

'Oh, I see,' Mark says. 'Because the Hindus have been sacrificing animals, the weather's been bad.'

He turns to me after Dawa has left.

'Why did we decide to do Baruntse during the Festival of Bad Weather?' he says.

'I didn't know these festivals were going to be on,

and nor did I know they brought bad weather.'

But Mark was continuing to think more creatively than me.

'There's one thing I don't understand,' he says. 'If it's so easy to bring on rain with a spot of Hindu bloodletting, why isn't it just as simple to conduct a Buddhist counter-puja to bring sunshine?'

I scratched my head.

'I don't know, Mark. Perhaps we should suggest it,' I reply.

DAY 8
THE GREAT BLACK MOUNTAIN

Wednesday, 20 October 2010 – Makalu Base Camp, Nepal

Mixed weather greets us in the morning. Angry grey clouds are swelling up from down the valley near Yangri Kharka, and it's clearly raining heavily somewhere down there. But up ahead, in the direction we're heading, there's blue sky and it looks altogether more pleasant. We've chosen to make an early start and are away by 7.30; we hope to get as far as we can towards Makalu Base Camp before the weather closes in.

There is a bit of porter difficulty again this morning. Dawa is nowhere to be seen and has apparently headed down-valley in the hope of finding more porters back at Yangri Kharka. The eight porters who leave camp this morning seem unsure what they're supposed to be carrying. Pasang notices a few bits and pieces they've left behind, and goes charging after them. He ends up carrying a tent himself, while Karma, one of our kitchen crew, carries

Mark's bag of climbing equipment.

While it's all being sorted out, Mark and I leave – slowly – with Sarki. It's the best day's trekking so far as we get in among the mountains. The path continues to rise steeply up the Barun Valley as the last vegetation gives way to true mountain scenery. The grass and dwarf rhododendron slowly thin, and soon all that remains is the odd clump of juniper as we reach a true glacial valley stacked up with banks of moraine. The southern side of the valley to our left is dominated by two pointed snow mountains – one an icy triangle directly above us, the other a narrow trapezium a little further on. I ask Sarki their names.

'I don't know, I'm sorry. This my first time here.'

This surprises me. Sarki is an old stager, who has worked as a cook for many trekking companies over the past 20 years. On previous treks, he has always known the trails better than anyone else.

'I thought you had been everywhere in Nepal, Sarki!' I say with a smile.

At the last teahouse before we leave civilisation, he asks an old man if he knows any local names for the peaks. He confidently tells us that the one marked on the map as Peak 7 – presumably because nobody has been able to find a local name for it – is called Pawune. Then he identifies two peaks that are unnamed on the map as Gombu-ma and Tsiring-ma.

If these are truly local names then why has nobody discovered them before – can we really be the first?

'We don't know how local "local" is,' Mark points out.

This is true. Gombu and Tsiring are both Sherpa first names – it's possible the old man has simply named them after his friends.

We continue boulder hopping beside a milk-white river, which is stacked up on the southern side by a huge bank of moraine. We catch up with Pasang, and at 10.30 we reach a large open area where the valley turns north towards Makalu Base Camp. This is marked on the map as Shershon, and is a popular camping spot.

Reaching moraine banks, with the mountain
known as Gombu-ma up ahead

It's starting to cloud over, and most of the peaks are partially obscured, but a small rock peak just peeps over a ridge. It seems unobtrusive from here, but Pasang assures us this is Makalu, the fifth highest mountain in the world.

By the time we reach camp, the rock peak is far from unobtrusive. For the next couple of weeks Makalu will tower above us like no other mountain, but the transformation is gradual. The English translation of Makalu is *great black mountain* – and we're about to find out why.

We rest for a while before continuing over boulders, and then among banks of grass. We come across Sarki resting in the sun at the bottom of a gully. He suggests we stop for lunch here, but he also tells us it's only an hour to camp; seeing the clouds welling up behind us, Mark and I choose to press on.

We reach Makalu Base Camp at 12.15. The approach is one of the most amazing vistas you could imagine. To our left the Barun Valley is far below us, and we look down upon the half dozen stone teahouses set among the flat, grey flood plain of the valley floor. Makalu is right in front of us now, a huge black rock face crowned by a sharp summit triangle, far higher above our heads than any other mountain we've seen today, its black face in stark contrast to the white snow peaks around it. This contrast is partly due to the steepness of Makalu's south face, which prevents it from holding snow. But it's also due to its size. It rises so prominently above the surrounding landscape that fierce winds batter its flanks and strip it clear of snow. But not all of it. In its lower portion, impossibly crinkled icefalls spill down to its base. It looks a truly frightening mountain from this angle.

Mark and I sit outside one of the teahouses at base

camp drinking tea and nibbling biscuits while we crane our necks towards the heavens. The statistics are worth noting, and occur to me even as I sit here. The summit of Makalu is no more than 5-6km away horizontally, but it stands at an altitude of 8,463m. Here at base camp we're at 4,800m. This means the summit is nearly 4km above us vertically.

I scan my memory to think of a comparably dominant mountain I may have seen before. The summit of Cho Oyu was only 2.5km above base camp in Tibet last month, and the giant south face of Lhotse towered 3km above me from the foot of Island Peak last year. I remember Muztagh Ata in western China. Its summit stands nearly 4km above the Xinjiang plateau, but the summit is so much more distant from its classic viewpoint at Lake Karakul. I remember that Mont Blanc, at 4,810m, stands nearly 4km above the town of Chamonix in the French Alps, but I don't remember it dominating the horizon like this. The harshness of Makalu's jagged black rock contrasts malevolently with the gentle white curves of Mont Blanc.

Barely an hour after we arrive, the clouds that have been chasing us up the Barun Valley all day finally catch up with us. By one o'clock Makalu is gone, only to reappear in windows that are all too brief. At lunch Mark and I discuss the possibility of resting for a day here. I could happily spend another day in this place if we're granted a better view tomorrow, and we agree to talk it through with Dawa.

Dawa arrives later in the afternoon from his

successful excursion to find more porters, and without prompting, he immediately suggests a rest day here as well. We agree.

I keep my fingers crossed for clear weather.

DAY 9
A TOUGH TREK FOR SOME

Thursday, 21 October 2010 – Makalu Base Camp, Nepal

But we don't have clear weather today, even for an hour, and Makalu remains firmly tucked away behind the clouds, accompanied by light snowfall for most of the day.

I get some clothes washed in the morning, but they don't have a chance to dry. I spend the rest of the day reading and chatting to Mark in the dining tent, which has been erected for the first time and furnished with a table and two chairs from the teahouse.

An elderly American group has arrived at base camp. They left behind one of their party in Yak Kharka when he fell off a bridge and injured himself. The Makalu Base Camp trek is a tough one by any standards, and evacuation from the Barun Valley, over Shipton's Pass and into the Arun Valley, is not easy. The group met Dawa yesterday during his search for new porters; they have come here in the hope of borrowing Mark's satellite phone to call a helicopter to evacuate their casualty.

'Typical bloody Americans, getting injured,' Mark says when he hears about it.

But this is just bravado and it masks his true generosity. When one of the group comes over at lunchtime to use the phone, he gives them advice and guidance – and although satellite phone calls are expensive, he won't hear of accepting any money when they offer it.

'Return the favour to someone else,' he says with a wave of his hand.

But when the helicopter flies overhead, the usual eerie clouds well up from lower down the Barun Valley, and (unfortunately for the injured trekker) the pilot is unable to land.

We've all been hoping that Mark's weather forecast is correct, and that today is the last of the bad-weather days. At 6pm we get our answer. All of a sudden the sky clears. There isn't a cloud to mask the peaks around us, although the sun has long since disappeared behind Tsiring-ma.

'It's a full moon,' Mark says. 'That usually brings new weather.'

It's very cold this evening, but we head for our sleeping bags in a more positive frame of mind. We don't get much sleep, though. Female company in the teahouse means our staff decide to hold a wild party. Banging Nepali music comes over from the teahouse, and although I shove in my ear plugs and drift off from time to time, I keep waking as the noisy beat drums in my ears.

DAY 10
IN THE SHADOW OF MAKALU

Friday, 22 October 2010 – Swiss Base Camp, Barun Glacier,
Nepal

I notice a light dusting of snow on the ground when Pasang opens the door of the tent to deliver bed tea at 6am. It's cold and frosty but clear outside – the first completely clear day we've had so far. This is the sort of autumn morning we've come to expect in Nepal, and it seems the weather really has turned a corner. When the sun comes out at seven o'clock, our mood improves considerably.

It seems to take our porters a long time to get organised this morning. While we wait, I wander up two small hills above base camp, expecting to find memorials to climbers who have lost their lives on Makalu. There are none, but the second hill has a fine view of the mountain across a dull green glacial lake. Makalu's crinkled black south face looks like a horrendous climb, as do the complex rocky ribs of the south-east ridge that lead up to the summit along our right-hand skyline. The left skyline looks more practical, descending gently to a snowy col. This col to the north is known as the Makalu La, and the ridge that leads from there to the summit has now become the standard route up Makalu.

Makalu turned out to be the bane of Edmund Hillary, the ambitious New Zealander who made the first ascent of Everest with Tenzing Norgay in 1953. The year after that great ascent, Hillary led a not-so-great (for him, anyway) expedition up the Barun Valley for the New Zealand Alpine Club. Their principal objective was Baruntse, but when they got to the upper end of the Barun Valley, a little beyond where we are now, they decided that Makalu might be feasible instead.

Alas for Hillary, by the time they made this decision, he had broken three ribs rescuing one of his teammates from a crevasse. He was having difficulty breathing and was clearly too weak to climb, but while the rest of his team pressed on up to 7,000m, establishing a series of camps as they climbed, he struggled in their wake. He eventually broke down trying to reach Camp 4 at 6,700m. His companions put him in a tent for two nights, but he became so weak that he could no longer descend on his own. He was strapped to a makeshift stretcher, and it took three days for him to be carried down to base camp.

Hillary later described his decision to push on as 'unbelievably stupid'. Stupid it may have been, but he went back to Makalu in 1961, suffered a stroke at Camp 3 and had to be evacuated again. The mountain ultimately cost him his talent as a high-altitude mountaineer, and he never climbed much higher than 6,000m again. His problems with altitude became so acute that in later life he would be reluctant to sleep above 2,500m.

Makalu was a traumatic place for Hillary, but the well-organised French team who made the first ascent in 1955 pretty much breezed up. They had pioneering one-piece down suits, 23 Sherpas and enough oxygen to use on high flow rates from low down on the mountain. They were also lucky enough to experience a number of calm and cloudless days around their summit attempt. They took the Makalu La route, but instead of ascending the ridge, they traversed onto the north face and set a high camp at 7,800m. Over the course of the next three days, the entire French team of eight climbers and their sirdar Gyalzen Norbu reached the top. The summit is said to be a tiny point no bigger than a yeti's paw, formed by three converging ridges.

The first two climbers to reach the summit were Lionel Terray and Jean Couzy. Both had also been part of the French team who made the infamous first ascent of Annapurna five years previously. This climb is famous for its epic rescue of the two summiteers Maurice Herzog and Louis Lachenal, who lost most of their fingers and toes to frostbite and needed to be trekked out on porter back. Terray himself suffered from snow blindness during the rescue on Annapurna, and his eyes were in agony for days. He later said of their ascent of Makalu that 'victory must be bought at a price of suffering and effort, and the clemency of the weather combined with the progress of technique had sold us this one too cheaply'.

Some people are just plain nuts.

We leave quite late, at 8.30, and follow a path leading to the foot of Makalu before turning left up the Barun Glacier. The path soon ends and we begin boulder hopping high to the left of the glacier. All the while, the giant black south face of Makalu looms over us, dauntingly bereft of snow. Gradually its shape changes as we round the corner – but it never looks any easier to climb.

Leaving Makalu Base Camp for the higher reaches of the Barun Valley, as Makalu towers overhead

At 11.30 we reach camp at 5,140m among giant boulders of moraine. The Barun Glacier is some distance below us, but across the valley Makalu now seems so close that we could reach out and touch it. It's hard to comprehend that its summit towers more than 3km above.

The place where we camp is known as Swiss Base Camp. Nobody seems to know why, but obviously a Swiss team must have camped here on their way to climb one of the surrounding peaks. This may have been an expedition in 1982, led by Romolo Nottaris. This particular expedition had two objectives: three members of the team tried to climb a new route on Makalu's west buttress and west face, which can be easily accessed from this camp, while the majority of the team went off to climb Baruntse like we are doing. They weren't the first to camp here, though. A photo from George Lowe's expedition report in the Alpine Journal shows that in 1954 Hillary's team from the New Zealand Alpine Club also camped very close to this spot.

To our left, a side glacier rises gently in front of a neat, symmetrical peak, unnamed on both our maps, but rising to 6,535m. Up this valley lies East Col, an alternative route onto the Barun Plateau. Our maps are confusing. I've come to realise over many years that Nepalese maps appear to be high quality with accurate contours, but they contain many errors. Features are often mislabelled. Names are incorrect, and places – usually villages – are plonked onto a trail at random, with no attempt to calculate their precise position. The trails are not precise either, making it hard to estimate distances.

In this case, the maps make a rather more fundamental error by confusing East Col with Sherpani Col and labelling the two passes the wrong way round. As its name implies, East Col is the most easterly (and southerly) of the two. Crossing it would mean a long walk across the Barun Plateau to reach West Col on the other side. We will be taking a more westerly side valley than this one, which snakes to the north and reaches the Barun Plateau further west at Sherpani Col.

East Col was actually the chosen col for Eric Shipton's 1952 Everest reconnaissance. On this, the second of two reconnaissance expeditions (the first being in 1951), Shipton's team decided to finish their expedition by crossing the Barun Plateau and exploring the Barun Valley. Charles Evans and two Sherpas, Da Tensing and Annullu, crossed East Col and tried to climb the 6,535m peak that I have just been admiring. They got to within 60m of the summit, but were stopped by a wide crevasse. Evans started to cross an exposed wall, expecting to be belayed by his Sherpa companions, but when he was halfway across he looked back and saw that one of them had his hands in his pockets and the other was exploring off in another direction. This put the willies up him and he decided to retreat.

Three days later, he returned with Eric Shipton, Edmund Hillary and George Lowe. When they reached the crevasse, Hillary saw things differently. There was a snow bridge that looked safe to him, so he nonchalantly strolled across where Evans had feared to tread. According to Hillary, Evans – who had now climbed the peak twice – looked mortified. But they all reached the summit.

Our maps are confusing me, but the geography to our north is also baffling. Both Mark and I think we are looking at the black rock face of Lhotse, and we believe the slightly higher snow peak to its right, standing further back, must be Everest. But this turns out to be an optical illusion. Every so often plumes of cloud further to the right reveal what looks to be an even higher mountain behind both of them, a knife edge of sheer rock.

A mountain higher than Everest? There's no such thing.

In fact, the white mountain lies in front of the black one, not behind it as we initially thought. It's 7,591m Shar Tse, while the black mountain is 8,382m Lhotse Shar (which doesn't qualify as one of the world's 8,000m peaks because it's just an outlier of Lhotse, and joined to it by the same ridge). Dawa tells us the big mountain behind both of them is 8,516m Lhotse, the fourth highest mountain in the world; and Everest, although close, cannot be seen.

The name Lhotse translates as *South Peak*, describing its proximity to Everest. Similarly Shar translates as *Ridge*, which tells us that Lhotse Shar is really no more than the summit ridge of Lhotse.

No mountaineer's journal is complete without references to toilet business, and mine is no different. We're having difficulties with our toilet tent. For the last two days it's been pitched on a surface of powdered rock that has been pounded by a glacier. Although this surface is a little more solid than sand, it's still somewhat unstable, and it crumbles at the sides as soon as anyone crouches over the pit. This creates a serious risk of falling in, and causes the pit to fill more quickly. The crew haven't been digging the pit very deep because only two of us are using it. When I give today's toilet its inaugural use, I nearly fill the pit at the first sitting.

DAY 11
BASE CAMP RECYCLING CENTRE

Saturday, 23 October 2010 – Sherpani Col Base Camp, Nepal

We have a slow start this morning. Although we wake at 6am, it's nearly 9am before we leave camp. Now that the sky is clear, this leisurely departure gives me time to study the skyline at the top end of the Barun Glacier.

I become more and more convinced that the mountain behind Lhotse Shar is in fact Everest, and not Lhotse. Everything about its profile is just right: the south-east ridge facing towards Lhotse Shar, the north-east ridge stretching some distance into Tibet, and the South Summit. The clinching factor is that there appears to be a massive drop between it and Lhotse Shar, not the couple of hundred metres there should be if the mountain were Lhotse. If only I had a map showing our present position with respect to Lhotse and Everest, then all would be clear.[3]

Today's trail begins by climbing high across

---

3 I'm eventually able to confirm that this mountain is indeed Everest.

boulders above camp. Occasionally there's a path, but mostly we scramble steeply over rocks. I end up getting my stick out to make things easier.

After about 150m of ascent the route flattens to traverse a short ridge, and we stop for a break. I'm reaching the conclusion that every day is getting better than the last. It doesn't matter how many times I come to Nepal; I can't help being dazed by the scenery. We're high above the Barun Glacier now. The landscape is wide open and desolate, but it possesses an uncluttered beauty that raises the spirit to such a level that it's almost overpowering. Makalu continues to dominate from the other side of the valley; it looks more and more climbable as we move across its base. Although steep, the west ridge looks far more inviting than any part of the mountain we've seen until now.

Everest holds me in its spell – a distance away yet, but still rising high above the top end of the glacier. We can even see Island Peak, nestling far below the giant rock wall of Lhotse Shar. It would be a substantial mountain anywhere else, but among these gargantuan towers it looks pathetic.

After a little more boulder hopping, the trail (if you can call it that) drops sharply around a corner into the side valley that leads up to Sherpani Col. The boulders here are very loose, and often clunk and shift as we move over them. Then Mark's right leg slips down a hole when he steps on a boulder that gives way. He cracks his knee and winces with pain. We stop for a few minutes to clean the wound with antiseptic wipes.

The trail is pretty much non-existent up this side valley as we climb steeply for some distance. Mark soldiers on, but I spare a thought for the porters, who are managing to keep up with us over this difficult terrain despite their huge loads. Eventually we round a corner to the right, the terrain flattens and we reach camp at 1pm.

Looking up at Lhotse Shar and Shar Tse,
as Everest peeps up to the right

The setting is impressive. Makalu still towers above and behind us, but ahead the scene has changed. An ice cliff bedecked with giant icicles rises about 50m above camp. Behind it a small pointed rock peak bars the way onto the Barun Plateau, but on each side of the peak is a pass, either one of which could be Sherpani Col, our gateway onto the plateau. A vertical rock face looming over us like a castle wall guards the south side of this steep valley. It's a fabulous setting here at 5,640m, but the surrounding walls of the valley are a little claustrophobic.

Mark's knee has lasted to here without swelling up, but it's still giving him pain. He's had his fair share of bad luck this expedition. His ribs have been giving him trouble ever since falling out of a rickshaw in Kathmandu, when the driver sped over a speed bump on our way home from Sam's Bar. I laughed raucously at that particular incident, but I didn't laugh today. The boulder was so large that any of us could have stepped on it thinking it to be stable. Had it rolled back and crushed his leg, heaven knows what sort of injury he might have received – and in a remote location where evacuation would be difficult to say the least.

We bask in the sun while the crew erect our tents below us. It's been another of those days worth living for. The campsite is to be our home for the next three nights, and the setting would be hard to match.

Unfortunately, it has also been home to people who haven't respected the beauty of the landscape around them. There's litter everywhere: empty food tins, old shoes, porter baskets, even a few old rusty tables. Unless anyone comes by here with the express intention of tidying, then this litter will never be picked up, since few expedition teams employ more porters than they need. Most of us only have enough to carry our own equipment and rubbish.

It's several days' walk over high passes to the nearest location where litter can be properly disposed of. On the other hand, it would be practical to incorporate litter-picking into an expedition's objectives without too many additional resources. It's common to send porters back as food gets eaten and expedition supplies diminish. Instead of paying them off and sending them back empty handed, they could be sent back with rubbish, as long as they were given the necessary instructions about how to dispose of it. There are probably several dozen loads here, though, so it would present a logistical challenge.

For now, our crew make the most of a bad job by appropriating one of the rusty tables for the dining tent and hiding its nastiness with a table cloth. They lay the rectangular metal porter baskets on their sides and put sleeping mats over them to make chairs. The dining and kitchen tents are joined together into one big tent with two rooms.

It's a civilised arrangement and much friendlier than previous camps. Now Mark and I can chat away to the guys in the next room as we have our dinner.

DAY 12
MONKLESS PUJA

Sunday, 24 October 2010 – Sherpani Col Base Camp, Nepal

Rest days sometimes seem to be busier than days when you're on the move. Such has been the case today, and we end up wondering where the time goes.

It was cold last night and I had to put more clothes on inside my 5-season sleeping bag to stay warm. At 6.30am it was -8°C inside the tent; by then it had warmed up sufficiently for me to loosen some of the drawstrings on the hood of my bag. For a two-man tent you can expect it to be a good ten degrees colder outside. I took a GPS reading this morning and discovered our altitude to be 5,700m. Mark and I both think that a night-time temperature of -20°C is very cold for this altitude. We can expect it to be even colder on summit day – perhaps -30°C without wind chill – and if this proves to be the case then we will be hoping for very light winds, or there will be a real risk of frostbite.

The crew have decided that today is an auspicious day to carry out our *puja* for the climb (a blessing ceremony to appease the mountain gods). But there are only six of us up here: me, Mark, Dawa, Pasang the guide, Sarki, and Karma (Pasang the kitchen assistant stayed down at Swiss Base Camp with the porters, ready for a second load-carry today). We don't have a monk to perform the ceremony, so we discuss which of us should take on the role. Obviously Mark and I can't do it because we're not Buddhists, but none of the others are keen to, either. They eventually decide on Karma, probably because he's the youngest and most junior. I approve of this choice, mainly because Karma the Lama sounds cool.

After breakfast, Dawa, Pasang and Karma build a cairn and attach three lines of prayer flags. Dawa has carried some pine clippings up from the forest zone to burn as incense. Various foodstuffs have been placed beside the cairn as offerings: biscuits, rice, bread, chocolate, tea, and the obligatory Sherpa Scotch whisky. The lack of a qualified monk means that it's one of the shortest puja ceremonies I've experienced, but as Mark remarks, it's the thought that counts (I've never seen a puja where a mountain god actually eats any of the food left for them either, so it must be the thought that counts here too). There's no chanting of mantras, but all the other essential elements of a puja are there. We toss rice to the wind, smear butter into our hair (or bald pate in my case), drink sugary tea and a few shots of whisky, part with some rupees as an offering, and leave our climbing equipment beside the shrine to be blessed by the mountain gods.

Our porters begin arriving from the lower camp while I'm doing my laundry after the puja. The two carries have given them a better chance to acclimatise, but I notice one of them is coughing, and remember that another was sick when we arrived in camp yesterday. These guys were born in the mountains and are used to carrying, and they tread the paths in flip-flops as easily as mountain goats, but it's easy to forget that we're travelling to an altitude that even they're not accustomed to. Mark and I are both acclimatised from previous expeditions, but some of our porters are not ready yet – and they still need to ascend another 400m to get us over the Barun Plateau into the Hongu Valley.

I ask Dawa to give the sick porters my Diamox and rehydration solution. It's much better for them to take it than for me to carry it and not use it, but Dawa decides one of them is too ill to go any higher, and he sends him back down.

In the afternoon, we prepare kit for our first day of climbing. We open the bags of technical equipment, get our axes, boots and crampons ready, and sort out our harness, prusik, jumar and carabiner systems in preparation for climbing.

DAY 13
THE BARUN PLATEAU

Monday, 25 October 2010 – Sherpani Col Base Camp, Nepal

Today is our first day of climbing as we head up to Sherpani Col for a spot of acclimatisation. It turns out to be a very cold day, but this is what we must be prepared for from now on.

We make a leisurely start again: a 7am wake-up, but we don't leave camp until 9.15. Pasang, Karma and one of the strongest porters leave before this – they want to break a porter route up to Sherpani Col by keeping to the moraine on the edges as much as possible, only joining the glacier when they have to. Although all three of them have crampons today, most of the porters will only be in boots, so the route on the glacier cannot be too steep. The glacier is also riddled with crevasses. It's important for Pasang, an experienced climbing guide, to find a safe route through and leave a trail for the porters to follow. They will not be roped together when we come to move camps.

Meanwhile, Dawa, Mark and I go straight onto the glacier from camp – we are roped together and have crampons. Getting onto it isn't so easy though. The snout rises as a 50m ice cliff straight out of base camp. It consists of very hard ice that is difficult to dig into with crampons, and it will be almost impossible to arrest with an ice axe in the event of a fall.

A shorter 20m section leads onto an easier snow ramp, so Dawa chooses to tackle this part. He walks up it with difficulty, going head-on up 50° slopes before turning to the right to bypass a short vertical section at the top. Here he anchors the rope with an ice screw and beckons me up.

The only way I can get up the first section is by front-pointing, as though I'm ice climbing, but when I come to turn right as Dawa did, my crampons hardly make a dent in the ice and I can't get any purchase. Dawa suggests I attach my jumar and haul myself directly up the vertical section instead. In this way I cruise to the top at the expense of a few aching arm muscles, and Mark follows.

From here the snow ramp leads easily onto the top of the glacier, and we find ourselves on a broad, flat snowfield that rises gently for some distance before steepening towards the crumbling rock cliffs guarding Sherpani Col.

I'm in the middle of the rope because I'm normally the slowest, so that Dawa can regulate our speed when he feels me tugging on the rope behind him. This time, however, my acclimatisation on Cho Oyu in Tibet has been considerably more helpful than

Mark's on Stok Kangri in India. I'm easily able to keep up with Dawa's pace at the front, but unkindly ignore Mark's tugging on the rope behind. After a while I hear some profanities behind me, and he shouts for us to slow down. From then on, we proceed across the snowfield at a more comfortable pace.

We walk non-stop for about an hour across the gentler snowfield, then pause for occasional short breaks as we climb the steeper sections. Halfway up, we see Pasang's party intersecting with us on our left. Dawa points out a safe way between crevasses, and we wait for them to catch us before ascending together.

It's cold and sunny. Every now and again an icy blast of wind reminds us that the weather is not as benign as we might think. The scenery is magnificent, most notably Makalu behind us, but it's not such a good day for photography – my camera battery is suffering from the cold. I have to keep taking the battery out to warm it in my hands before I can use the camera. Even then I can only take two pictures before the camera flashes red and powers off.

We reach the foot of the rock cliffs beneath Sherpani Col at about 11.30. It's been easy until now, but 80m of tricky snow and rock now guard the top of the pass. Pasang, Karma and the porter need to cross the pass and leave their loads at Camp 1 on the other side. Dawa, Mark and I agree to climb up to the pass before turning around, but as we're setting off Mark decides to unrope and wait for us at the bottom.

I can understand his point as I climb a short snow slope at the base of the climb. I'm only crossing a thin layer of snow on top of crumbling rocks and have hardly any purchase with my crampons. Were I to fall when roped to Mark, there would be nothing to stop both of us tumbling all the way down onto jagged boulders at the foot of the cliff. It gets a little easier above the snow slope, but there's still no margin for error.

A short diagonal rock climb leads onto steep crumbling slopes. Here, as well as keeping my own sure feet, I have to worry about the additional hazard of kicking loose rocks onto Pasang's team below me. There's a worrying moment when the porter decides to stop for a rest directly beneath our line of ascent. For about 5m of climbing I have to crouch down, crab-like, alert for any loose rocks I dislodge so that I can stop them crashing down onto our friends.

I'm relieved when I see prayer flags ahead of me. We reach the top of the pass without mishap.

We are greeted by a hidden world: a huge snow plateau guarded by snow peaks and ridges, one of which we're perched upon. To the left, beyond the plateau, Hinku Chuli is most prominent, rising in a wall of snow and rock 700m above the plateau. Ahead, there's a gap in the wall of mountains: West Col and our eventual route down into the Hongu Valley to join up with our route between Mera and Island Peaks last year. Behind this gap, on the far horizon, is another line of more distant mountains; and in front of it, just above West Col, are six small two-man tents. This is Camp 1, and the only evidence of the 18 expedition teams that are supposed to be on Baruntse this year. To the right a pyramid of snow marked on the map as 6,752m watches like a sentinel over the plateau. This is by far the most prominent peak in view, and yet neither of my maps gives it a name. Peeking up sheepishly behind it is a narrow trapezoid sliver of snow – the summit of Baruntse.

This vast sea of ice is known as the Barun Plateau. It was named by Eric Shipton and Edmund Hillary, who saw it for the first time when they crested West Col during their 1951 Everest reconnaissance expedition. It's hard to take a photograph of this panorama, as no single aspect draws the attention, so instead I sweep around and try to take a video. But before my camera's been on for 60 seconds, the warning light comes on and the battery goes out. It's so cold that a single camera battery hasn't even lasted a day.

Behind me the contrast is dramatic. Makalu takes up almost the entire view, the smooth snow plateau we've just crossed spreading itself across the foreground like a white sheet.

Another rock barrier guards the way down to the Barun Plateau – perhaps a little shorter than the one we've just climbed, but just as tricky. Dawa descends a short distance to fix ropes and help Pasang lower the porter loads down to the plateau. I find a precarious seat above them and watch for a while, but there's not much shelter up here and the wind bites at my feet. In the end I spend an hour on the col. When

Dawa returns, I'm marching on the spot to keep warm. By then the three dots of Pasang's group are halfway across the plateau to Camp 1.

I haven't been looking forward to the descent, and we ease our way down carefully. At times I lower myself down the rock on all fours, but it isn't until we reach the snow slope that I have trouble. I know that a slip here will mean at best nasty injuries for me and Dawa, and at worst mashing ourselves to a pulp on the jagged rocks below. I can no longer find the steps we used on the way up (these were precarious in any case). It's not until Dawa finds a position from where he can belay me that I'm able to descend with confidence. We reach Mark at the bottom of the rock face just as the sun drops behind Sherpani Col and he's disappearing into shadow. It's two hours since we left him; he's done well to keep warm.

We return across the snow slopes to base camp quickly and easily, and reach camp just before three o'clock.

In the evening we discuss our plans for the next few days. We have seven days left to climb Baruntse, but the forecast Mark has received by satellite phone from his girlfriend Claire is not promising. As I stood in the wind on Sherpani Col, I knew that today was not a summit day. Claire's forecast confirms there were 45km per hour winds at 6,500m. These are extremely high for that altitude, and it would be bleak sheltering in our tents at Camp 1 in those conditions. The winds are forecast to drop to 25km per hour on Friday and Saturday. This is just about a summit window, on the fringes of doable, although the cold temperatures we're experiencing would make it a bitter one. We will need to be careful about frostbite.

We decide to have another rest day here in Sherpani Col Base Camp tomorrow, and keep our fingers crossed the winds drop even more on Sunday and Monday – our last opportunities to climb Baruntse. It's been a bleak and hopeless forecast until now, but the slightly lower winds offer a glimmer of hope.

Mark and I discuss our prospects in our tent.

'Just like you have to be prepared for bad weather and change your plans,' he says, 'you have to be prepared for good weather as well, and make a dash for the summit if there's an opportunity.'

Although the forecast isn't great, we'll continue with our preparations as though it is.

DAY 14
BASE CAMP LASSITUDE

Tuesday, 26 October 2010 – Sherpani Col Base Camp, Nepal

We have a lazy day today, likely to be the easiest for many days. We're woken up with bed tea at 8am, well after the sun has risen, and I lie idly in my sleeping bag until breakfast is called half an hour later. I barely leave the dining tent all morning as I read, write up my diary, and discuss potential future mountaineering objectives with Dawa. I'm still there when lunch is called and only leave at two o'clock. By this time I've drunk enough tea to hydrate a small army.

After lunch, I decide to go for a short walk up the ridge behind base camp.

'I'm going to do exactly what it says on the tin,' Mark says as I'm getting ready, 'and use a rest day for resting.'

My walk turns out to be a bad idea. The route is on loose rock, and everything I step on moves. I turn back a long way short of the ridge after deciding it's not safe. Even then I have to tiptoe carefully on the way down. To be crushed under a pile of boulders after sliding 20m in a rock avalanche triggered by my own clumsiness... That would not be a good ending. I would be a candidate for the Darwin Awards. It's a relief when I get back down to camp without mishap, barely 45 minutes after setting out.

As has happened every day at base camp, a lethargy comes over me as soon as the sun slips behind the rocks of Sherpani Col at four o'clock. I feel tired and lack motivation. When afternoon tea has ended, I creep back to our tent and tuck myself up in my sleeping bag. I know this lethargy will last until dawn 14 hours later. In W.E. Bowman's classic comic novel about mountaineering, *The Ascent of Rum Doodle*, this phenomenon is known as 'base camp lassitude'.

DAY 15
OVER SHERPANI COL

Wednesday, 27 October 2010 – Camp 1, Barun Plateau, Nepal

We have an early start today for the crossing of Sherpani Col, but Mark and I are so used to waiting in the cold for breakfast that when we're woken at 6am we lie and rest for 20 minutes before making a move.

I discover that the reason for these late starts is our diminishing supply of porters. When they leave camp at 7.30 I count just six of them. A few days ago, at Makalu Base Camp, we had 13.

'Where have all our porters gone?' I ask Dawa.

He explains that we started out with 30, but he sent them back as we used up our supplies or they became ill.

'But we can't have eaten 24 porters-worth of food?' I ask in amazement.

'Yes, that's right. We have.'

There is probably some sort of logarithmic function that enables you to calculate the amount of food needed for a party of mountaineers trekking across remote terrain, but you need to be a mathematician to make sense of it. Trekking sirdars like Dawa, however, seem able to carry it in their heads. It goes something like this: for every porter who carries equipment, you need porters to carry food for them. And then you need more food for the porters who are carrying food, which means yet more porters. W.E. Bowman summed it up in *The Ascent of Rum Doodle*:

> *Five porters would be needed for this. Two porters*
> *would be needed to carry food for these five, and*
> *another would carry food for these two. His food*
> *would be carried by a boy. The boy would carry his*
> *own food. The first supporting party would be*
> *established at 38,000 feet ... which necessitated*
> *another eight porters and a boy. In all ... three*
> *thousand porters and three hundred and seventy-five*
> *boys would be required.*

Our six remaining porters make a surprise start. Instead of taking the route to Sherpani Col reconnoitred by Pasang two days ago, they climb high on loose rock to the right of the glacier, joining it on the route taken by Dawa, Mark and me. Since they all confidently go the same way, they must have discussed it with Pasang prior to departure, but the loose rocky terrain is similar to the stuff I rejected as unsafe yesterday. The danger is compounded by the fact that the rubble crosses above an ice cliff; were any of the porters to trigger a rock slide they would be carried over it. I watch for several minutes with my heart in my mouth as one by one they make it across this section safely.

Dawa, Mark and I leave camp at 8.20 and stride more confidently up the short ice cliff at the snout of the glacier. By the time we're onto the broad snow slope up to Sherpani Col, all of the porters are some way ahead of us, except for one who is still struggling across the loose rock with his load. Sarki is waiting for him. We move on, but when we stop for water we see Sarki carrying the porter's load up the glacier behind us. The porter is ill with fever and a headache – clear symptoms of altitude sickness – and it's not safe for him to continue up to the Barun Plateau with us. Sarki dumps the load on the glacier and goes back down to fetch his own kit.

We're now down to just five porters, three kitchen crew and two guides. Of the 30 porters we started with, 13 have gone back because of illness. Mark and I are acclimatised from previous expeditions, and this is the first time I've found myself coping with altitude better than our Nepali staff.

'Are we doing this trek too quickly?' I ask Dawa.

'No, it's because the porters are not as good,' Mark says.

Dawa nods in agreement.

This autumn is the busiest I've seen it in Nepal. Porters are at a premium. Dawa tried to secure the fantastic porters we had on Mera and Island Peaks last year, but at the last minute those who agreed to come were offered more money by other groups.

Previously the 1,000 rupees a day plus food that we're paying them would have been considered good wages, but not this season. Some of these porters were offered 1,500 rupees a day, so we can't really blame them for deserting us.

We're doing one of the toughest treks in Nepal with what porters Dawa has been able to rustle up at the last minute. And the hardest part of the trek is about to come.

Reascending the Sherpani Col Glacier, with the cliffs of Sherpani Col up ahead

We reach the top of the snow slope, and arrive at the foot of the rock cliffs guarding Sherpani Col at 11am. This is where we really find out what our five remaining porters are made of. Treading with the greatest of care, Dawa, Mark and I creep up the short, steep section of snow at the base of the cliff. A slip here would be very nasty indeed. It's hard enough for us, but looking back we now see our porters completing the same journey with heavy loads secured to their backs by means of a tumpline across their foreheads. I'd hate to be in their shoes. All we can do is hold our breaths and keep our fingers crossed for them.

I always feel alarmed when I see Nepalese porters carrying heavy loads up a steep slope using tumplines. Broken necks or strangulation would appear to be the likely outcome of a fall. I certainly wouldn't be able to do it; my neck simply isn't strong enough, but tumplines aren't dangerous for people who have been using them all their lives. The outdoor equipment manufacturer Patagonia even started selling tumplines in 1980 after its founder Yvon Chouinard found that they prevented the long-term back problems he experienced when using backpacks. During an expedition to Nepal in 1978, he noticed how the local porters had all developed muscles down both sides of their spinal columns, and he realised that their necks must be as strong as their shoulders.

We scramble up the remaining rock to the top of the pass at 6,180m, but we don't linger here – it's going to take some time to get all the loads over. Pasang the guide is climbing in front of us, and has fixed a series of ropes across the rock face on the far side of the pass, where the trail angles gradually downwards. We attach our carabiners to them and slowly climb down. I've chosen to keep my crampons on, which makes things harder for me.

Towards the bottom of the rock face a tongue of ice spills down onto the Barun Plateau. Dawa lowers us vertically down this section, and two out of twelve of us are across the pass safely.

It's twelve o'clock. For the next three hours Mark and I sit on the plateau and watch as, one by one, our loads – and then people – are lowered down to the plateau. We're so short of porters that it takes several relays, and someone needs to go all the way back down the glacier to retrieve the load left there by Sarki. Everyone contributes – except for me and Mark as we sit and film it all. Pasang the guide, Sarki the cook, Pasang and Karma the kitchen assistants carry just as many loads as the porters. Several times, Dawa leaves his place at the top of the ice cliff where the loads are being lowered, heads back up to the pass, and disappears over the other side before reappearing with a load across his forehead.

Some of the guys are more confident than others. Some are quite happy arm-wrapping Nepali style down the fixed ropes, and positively run up and down them when unencumbered, but others get nervous. One of them dislodges a huge rock, which clatters down the cliff face to land just below where Mark and I are waiting safely on the glacier. Spooked, the porter sits down where he dislodged the rock, and waits until one of his more confident colleagues notices him and comes back up to help with the load.

We have other distractions while we sit and while

away the time. Behind us, the wide expanse of snow that is the Barun Plateau stretches across the near horizon, surrounded by mountain walls. We look across to Camp 1 on the other side of the plateau and watch figures wander between the tents. Right of here, the route up to Camp 2 on Baruntse angles up a 30° snow slope between two pointed snow peaks. The nearer of the two peaks hides Baruntse's bulk. We watch figures coming down the slope, perhaps from trips to Camp 2 or summit attempts, but again today seems much too cold and windy for a good opportunity to reach the top.

We study the unnamed 6,535m mountain rising above East Col to see if there's a realistic route to the summit. We compare East Col and adjacent Sherpani Col, which we've chosen to cross, to try and understand why Sherpani Col has become the favoured crossing. Gentle snow slopes rise up to East Col. Sherpani Col just seems to cross a random point on a rock wall. It doesn't look like a pass at all, but it's much closer to West Col, our exit point from the Barun Plateau. We also don't know the condition of the side valley leading up to East Col. We had a lot of uncomfortable boulder hopping to do up our valley, and Mark injured his leg, but the glacier was straightforward. Perhaps the route on the other side of East Col presents more of a challenge?

At one point Mark looks behind us and says, 'Am I going mad?'

I turn around and see that a yellow tent seems to have appeared halfway across the plateau. Neither of us had noticed it before. A few seconds later it turns upside down and begins bouncing down the glacier, and we watch it spinning round and round until it ends its journey by disappearing into a crevasse.

'If you are, then we're both mad,' I reply.

'Yeah,' Mark grunts, suppressing a laugh. 'That's definitely true.'

The wind gusts intermittently. It's pleasant when calm, but the gusts are random and violent, and when they hit us it becomes bitterly cold. By three o'clock they have become more frequent. Since all but three of our team are safely across and heading to Camp 1, we decide to follow them.

We walk towards the sun as it gently drops towards the jagged horizon in front of us. It's a pleasant walk, but we soon discover that a gale is blowing at Camp 1 on the plateau at 6,140m. We squeeze into one of the tents that Sarki and the team have set up. Only now do we realise we have a dilemma: it's much too windy to set up the porter tent, but it's a long way down over West Col to a safe place below the plateau. Less than three hours of daylight remain. I personally don't fancy moving from this spot for another long walk, but the porters crowded into the other tent are looking glum.

But the matter is quickly resolved when Dawa arrives. Baruntse is his second home, and he has many friends among the climbing Sherpas here. One of them, travelling with another team, is descending anyway. He offers to escort the porters and kitchen crew down to his camp for the night. Dawa, Pasang and Sarki remain in the second tent at Camp 1 while Mark and I settle into ours.

'They're good lads,' I remark, as I hear someone securing our tent pegs more firmly against the howling wind.

They've all relayed big loads today to cover our porter shortage, and still they are doing everything they can to make us comfortable.

Sarki cooks up soup and pasta next door, and Pasang brings it to our tent. Despite the howling wind, we settle comfortably into our sleeping bags for 14 hours of rest.

DAY 16
THE STICKLEBACK RIDGE

Thursday, 28 October 2010 – Baruntse Base Camp, Nepal

We make a late start this morning at 8am. It turns out to be another long and busy day. Having unpacked all our kit last night, we pack it up again this morning to be carried down to a new base camp on the west side of the Barun Plateau. It's much too cold and windy at Camp 1 to be spending any longer here than we have to, and we need to keep our strength up for the climb.

In preparation for this, Dawa, Mark and I rope up and leave for Camp 2 shortly before ten o'clock. A well-established trail leads up snow slopes between Baruntse's two unnamed southern peaks. I'm feeling fit thanks to my acclimatisation on Cho Oyu last month; I easily keep up with Dawa as he leads the way at the front of the rope, but behind me Mark is finding the pace a little too quick. We have to stop regularly for him to get his breath back; and once again I am treated to a generous dose of vernacular

English as he voices his displeasure at the pace.

We now have a perfect position to look down onto the Barun Plateau. It's an amazing hidden sanctuary: a natural amphitheatre at 6,000m, surrounded by a ring of jagged peaks. I feel like I am standing on the upper circle, looking down on the arena below. The surface is smooth as a kitchen work surface, with an apparent absence of giant cracks (although there must be many deep crevasses). Rarely have I seen such a huge expanse of white.

The New Zealand team who made the first ascent of Baruntse in 1954 camped somewhere on the plateau after crossing East Col. In his report for the Alpine Journal, George Lowe said they camped just below the saddle that leads to the Hongu Valley, and had glorious views of Makalu and Lhotse. But this must have been a mistake. The saddle can only have been West Col, which meant they camped in roughly the same position as we had. While Makalu rises clearly above the rock wall of Sherpani Col, any view of Lhotse is blocked by the towering snows of Baruntse and its outliers.

After establishing another camp at 6,700m on a small col below Baruntse (quite a lot higher than the Camp 2 that we are heading towards), Lowe, Bill Beaven, Geoff Harrow and Colin Todd set off for the summit at 6am the following morning. This was a very late start; a little too late as things transpired. As they were traversing a flatter, corniced section of the summit ridge, Beaven – who was climbing with Lowe – stuck his ice axe into the snow and watched in horror as a crack opened at his feet and a 60m section of ice snapped off and fell down Baruntse's east face. Lowe hurled himself towards the west side of the ridge to provide a counterbalance on the rope should Beaven fall down the face. But when there was no tug on the rope, he turned around and saw Beaven standing on the brink, unharmed.

'That was close,' Beaven said with a grin.

The fright probably made the two men nervous. They continued for a few hours more, but when the weather deteriorated in the dimming afternoon light, they decided to turn around and head back to camp. Harrow and Todd continued to the summit, but didn't reach it until 4.30pm. They reached the top in swirling cloud and could see nothing of the view. When they descended they found that the wind and snow had covered the many hundreds of steps they had cut on the ascent. They lost their way, and didn't get back to camp until long after dark. Lowe and Beaven returned to climb Baruntse two days later, but they too found the summit in cloud.

We are climbing in much better conditions today, with blue sky overhead, but Dawa is deep in thought.

'Do you know name of Sherpa who climb Everest nineteen times?' he asks out of the blue during one of our rest breaks.

'Apa Sherpa has climbed it the most, but I think he's climbed it twenty times,' I reply. 'In my team on Cho Oyu last month was Mingma Sherpa, who has climbed it sixteen times. I think he's fourth on the all-time list. Why do you ask?'

'The one who climb it nineteen times. He die up there,' Dawa replies, pointing towards Baruntse.

'What, not recently?' I ask.

'About five, six day ago. They still not find the body.'

'What happened?'

'Not sure. I think avalanche.'

I'm stunned. Climbing Sherpas are paid handsomely in comparison to their peers, and their wages from mountaineering are sufficient to support extended families, but the job is not free from danger. Somewhere down in the Khumbu region, there is a family facing up to a vanishing income while grieving for a loved one. Every death is a tragedy, but if what Dawa has told us is true then this one will be felt more widely. Sherpas who have climbed Everest multiple times are celebrities in their community; one who has climbed it 19 times must be a legend.

More immediately for us, it puts a new angle on the hazards we are facing. We thought the problem was going to be the wind, but now it seems that snow conditions on the summit ridge may not be safe.

The leader of the Adventure Peaks expedition team reinforces this point when he passes us on the way down with his group.

'I hear there's been a bit of snow up there,' I say to him.

'It's not just the amount, it's the condition of the snow. Look...'

He steps off the path to put his foot into the snow to the side. It's a solid crust on top with fine powder underneath. These are just the sort of conditions that created a severe avalanche risk for my team on Cho Oyu last month, and it looks like it's going to be the same all over again.

Eventually the path levels out as we pass between the two snow peaks into a flattish bowl. Baruntse rises 700m above us, not so much a whaleback as a stickleback ridge, narrow in places, with many crests and troughs along its length. We've been watching two figures make their way up the near end of it. They're now on their way down again, having turned around a long way short of the lowest summit at our end of the ridge.

We reach Camp 2 in the bowl, 6,425m, at 11.45am. Baruntse doesn't seem so very far above us now. On the first ascent, Geoff Harrow and Colin Todd took more than ten hours to reach the summit from a camp much higher than this one. It seems sluggish, but in those days climbers were still rejecting crampons in favour of the old-fashioned technique of step cutting. After Bill Beaven broke a slab of mountain off with his ice axe, Colin Todd took over the lead and spent another two hours hacking away at the slope with his axe to build a staircase of steps – steps that had been filled in by snow by the time they came to descend. What an exhausting waste of time.

'Sorry we've had to keep stopping,' Mark says, 'but I can't keep up with you two.'

But Dawa says that two hours from Camp 1 is a very good time, so to do it in only one hour 45 minutes on our first ascent bodes well. It's not that

Mark's been struggling; Dawa and I have been flying.

We walk a little beyond Camp 2 to get fine views down into the Hongu Valley to the west, where our new base camp will be pitched, and which all three of us traversed last year on our way between Mera and Island Peaks. I have happy memories of that section of the trek.

Approaching Camp 2 with Baruntse's summit up ahead

Beyond Camp 2 the trail rises steeply to another col between Baruntse and the right-hand snow peak, before turning left to scale the front face of Baruntse in what looks like a non-technical snow slog. At 12.15 we decide to turn around. We descend rapidly to the plateau, as though we are descending the stairs of the auditorium, and we're back at Camp 1 just half an hour later.

Our porters are assembling here to begin the task of relaying equipment over West Col to our new base camp. Mark and I shelter in our tent for a couple of hours while Sarki cooks up soup and black tea. When Dawa returns at three o'clock to say the relay has been completed, it's freezing outside and the wind has been buffeting against our tent for a while. I get frozen fingers putting on my crampons. They don't warm up again for quite some time.

West Col turns out to be a very different proposition to Sherpani Col, but every bit as demanding. I don't know exactly what I was expecting – perhaps an easy snow slope – but on the other side of a snow mound behind Camp 1, I find myself facing a 100m abseil down 60° snow slopes. It's going to be a challenge to get back up again. How on earth did they get the porters down here with their loads? I'm grateful to complete this section with my harness, abseil device and safety carabiner. Our porters had none of these things, and will have needed to descend by means of an arm wrap. This can be an effective and safe technique for descending a fixed rope. It involves wrapping the fixed rope around your arm as you descend. You can slide your arm down the rope, and the friction of the rope provides a break to slow your descent. It also provides protection: if you fall, the weight of your body will cause your arm to catch in the rope and you will fall no further. But you need to be confident and experienced to deploy this technique. When we watched them descending Sherpani Col yesterday, we could see that many of our crew could arm wrap as easily as carrying a basket, but one of the porters was less confident.

At the bottom of the snow slope there is a short overhanging rock section, which means I must finish my abseil with a leap of faith. Mark is less keen on abseiling since sustaining first-degree burns on his hands after setting fire to his tent on Aconcagua (a story that is best told another time). Thanks to the injury, he now finds it much harder to grip a rope. Instead of jumping over the overhang, he takes an alternative route off to the left, where ropes have been fixed down some rocky slabs. An abseil necessitates gripping the rope with your hands to prevent a freefall. But Mark demonstrates that he is also an accomplished arm-wrapper, and gets down the slabs easily.

It's been an interesting descent so far, but this was just the start of it. We rope up again and descend a beautiful series of buttresses and snow plateaus towards the setting sun, with Ama Dablam and other breathtaking mountains silhouetted before us. When the sun disappears behind a ridge and we drop below the snow line onto moraine, Dawa runs ahead to help set up camp, leaving Mark and me to complete the descent in dimming light.

Initially we go to the wrong campsite, and squint through the darkness trying to recognise our tents. Our cries of 'Dawa!' meet with no response, but then we spot another campsite beside a lake, and we head towards it, stumbling across a boulder field in pitch blackness. Pasang rushes past us carrying our two duffle bags, which he snatched from a tiring porter, determined to get them to camp ahead of us.

When I find Dawa trying to put our tent up in the dark, I fish my head torch out of my pack and lend a hand. It's a makeshift campsite that has been erected in dimming light, but everything we need is here, and it feels warmer and more comfortable than any camp we've stayed in for days. We're even able to keep our door open this evening as they bring a lovely plate of fried rice and omelette to our tent.

It's been another long day, but we curl up in our sleeping bags and go to sleep in the happy knowledge that we have a rest day ahead of us.

DAY 17
THE TRAGEDY OF CHEWANG NIMA

Friday, 29 October 2010 – Baruntse Base Camp, Nepal

We wake to find ourselves camped on a beach beside a silvery lake that shimmers in the breeze. The majestic granite wall of Baruntse's west face towers overhead beyond the lake, painted carefully with giant streaks of ice. From the northern end of the Hongu Valley, Baruntse is one of a pair of towering ice mountains rising above a desert of moraine. On the left, trapezoidal Kali rises to 6,985m. Its southern face is almost completely white with organ pipes of fluted ice. Baruntse is joined to Kali by a jagged ridge, rising more than 6,500m throughout its length. Baruntse's outline is gentler than Kali's – its summit could almost be described as the high point on the ridge before it falls away more steeply to a flatter horizon at West Col. Baruntse's face is more rocky than Kali's, suggesting that it's steeper. There's no doubt about it, base camp on the west side of the Barun Plateau is a much more welcoming setting than the east side, which was hemmed in by rock walls and the threatening mass of Makalu.

The crew bring bed tea at 8am, and Sarki lays out a sleeping mat in front of our tent, where he serves us breakfast. We wolf down scrambled egg and pancakes while we gaze across the lake at our objective. The sun is warm and our campsite is sheltered from the wind. I sit on the mat all morning and feel no inclination to move.

Pasang points out two tiny specks crawling up Baruntse's summit ridge, traversing the first of four summits at about the point we saw the two figures turn around yesterday. Yesterday's climbers decided the ridge was too dangerous; it will be interesting to see how today's fare.

Baruntse's west face from base camp

Dawa arrives from his networking around camp and explains the situation. The two climbers on the ridge are Sherpas fixing ropes for the SummitClimb team. After the accident that happened a few days ago, we weren't sure if the summit ridge would be safe for people to go back up, or whether this was just an isolated accident. It now seems that Sherpas from SummitClimb have decided that it's safe enough, though I guess there is still some avalanche risk.

Dawa tells us a little more about the tragedy. The Sherpa's name was Chewang Nima. He was fixing ropes close to the summit for his client, an American woman,[4] when he dropped through a cornice on the Makalu side. As he fell, his rope caught around a section of solid ice, then snapped. He plummeted to his death.

'That sounds like a summit bonus problem,' Mark says. 'Commercial groups would say if it's not safe for us it's not safe for Sherpas, but a single climber, rich, American, offering a lot of money to fix ropes up there... You know, you can never be sure, but you could definitely give it that interpretation.'

'You could. But a single climber is also likely to be more experienced,' I reply.

'Yeah, we're guessing I know. He's also climbed Everest nineteen times, so he can make his own decisions.'

In my heart of hearts, I know that it's a dangerous thing to try and climb these Himalayan mountains. At

4 We discover later that the client is Melissa Arnot, an experienced mountain guide who has herself climbed Everest multiple times.

some point, each of us has to take a calculated risk, and sometimes we are just unlucky. On the first ascent of Baruntse, Bill Beaven found himself standing on the edge of a cornice after slicing a section off with his ice axe. If the cornice broke off to his right then I assume he must have been carrying the axe in his right hand, or he would have been standing on the cornice when it broke. But it's normal practice to carry your axe on the uphill side, which in this case would have meant carrying it in his left hand. In other words, he survived because he was doing the wrong thing. He was a very lucky man.

Chewang Nima wasn't so lucky. He was standing on the cornice when it broke, and it cost him his life.

At some point, we are going to have to make a decision about whether to take the risk. Is the summit ridge safe to climb? We keep our eyes on the Sherpas up there today. If they can get close to the summit, then maybe it is. In any case, we don't have many options – our flights from Lukla are a week on Tuesday, and we still have a five-day trek to get there. Dawa suggests we have another rest day tomorrow, then on Sunday we go to Camp 2 in preparation for a summit attempt on Monday. The rest is in the lap of the mountain gods.

Sarki has got hold of fresh buffalo meat and we have fried buffalo wrapped in chapati for lunch. It's delicious, but then I go too far by asking for peanut butter to spread on my last chapati. Our supplies are in one place for the first time in days. Sarki goes through them all looking for a single jar, but to no avail.

Face sombre, Dawa comes to report the bad news. 'I'm sorry, Mark, but we don't have peanut butter.'

'Perhaps it's still up there,' says the other Mark, pointing towards West Col. 'I think you should send one of the boys up to have a look.'

We laugh.

After lunch, Mark and I reminisce about the countries we've visited to climb mountains. We talk about Ecuador, where I was last Christmas.

'Do you know the Panama hat originated in Ecuador?' I ask.

'Yes,' he replies, 'but do you know how it got its name?'

I remain silent, kicking myself. I'd forgotten that Mark has a mind for useless trivia.

'It was the favoured headgear of Ferdinand de Lesseps when he was building the Panama Canal. All of the photos of the canal's construction in the early days featured his hat, so even though it came from Ecuador people called it the Panama hat.'

There's a five-second pause, and I think he's finished, but he hasn't.

'And did you know that the way to test if it's a genuine Panama hat is to roll it up into a tube and insert it through a ring? When it comes out the other side it should retain its shape.'

Another pause – I'm not sure how to reply.

'So, yes, I did know the Panama hat comes from Ecuador,' he says.

I'm sorry I asked.

The performance of the rope-fixing team high on the ridge has offered a glimmer of hope, but just before dinner Mark notices wispy cirrus clouds high overhead. This is usually the harbinger of bad weather; we can expect a storm to begin some time in the next 24 hours, just when we hope to begin our summit attempt.

After dinner, Dawa comes to the dining tent in a brooding mood. He's been talking to some of the other Sherpas in camp. They're upset that Chewang Nima's body is still lying somewhere over the Makalu side of Baruntse, and they say nobody has sent a helicopter to look for it.

'If this was westerner,' he says, 'they would send helicopter straight away to recover body. Lowest porter or richest client – all should be treated same.'

We can't argue with the sentiment, but Dawa isn't entirely correct about westerners. I know that our trekking agency, The Responsible Travellers, has provided insurance for all of our crew, including the porters, but I have to confess that I don't know the full details of what it covers, including the amount. I suspect that it would only cover an evacuation of someone at serious risk, rather than an extensive search for someone already believed to be dead. In the case of insurance for tourists, most mountaineering insurance policies cover search and rescue, including helicopter evacuation. Some, however, only cover rescue from a known location, without the search element. Most policies do not cover the search and recovery of a body from a remote mountain location, and often a victim's family has to pay for this themselves. These costs can be considerable; sometimes money is raised online through crowdfunding.[5]

Dawa is upset, though, and I can see that now is not the time to argue the point.

In any case, I have to remind myself how easily rumours can spread at an expedition base camp; all stories need to be taken with a pinch of salt until they are verified. At the moment, the only thing we're sure of is that Chewang Nima died a few days ago. Everything else is speculation. The most likely scenario is that both client and Sherpa weighed the risks and took their chances, but sometimes in the mountains the dice land badly.

---

5 In fact, we learn that helicopters were sent to look for Chewang Nima's body, but conditions meant that it was considered too dangerous to carry out an extensive search.

DAY 18
A RAY OF SUNSHINE

Saturday, 30 October 2010 – Baruntse Base Camp, Nepal

Things seem to be going tits up again. We're sitting on sleeping mats in the dining tent eating our breakfast, and Mark is checking messages on his satellite phone, as he often does.

'Hmm...' he says, 'forecast for Sunday: light snow at 5,500m, heavy snow in the afternoon. Winds 25km an hour, temperature -21°C. Monday clear, more snow on Tuesday.'

Hmm, indeed. If this forecast proves accurate then we're stuffed – and there's no reason to suppose it won't be. We saw the cirrus clouds last night, and even as we're having breakfast, undulating folds of altostratus are racing by overhead and blotting out the sun. The only thing not quite right about Mark's forecast is the temperature of -21°C, which seems implausible.

We discuss this news with Dawa. Although it significantly diminishes our chances of success, it doesn't change our plans by much. Monday remains our only summit window, and to give us that chance we have to climb high tomorrow in the light-to-heavy snow. The only change Dawa suggests is to go to Camp 1 rather than Camp 2, as Camp 1 is already established, and setting up Camp 2 is going to be difficult in the heavy snow predicted for tomorrow afternoon. Although this will mean a longer summit day, it makes sense.

There's an alternative plan. Now that climbing Baruntse seems an unlikely prospect, we could not bother going up at all, and instead do some exploratory trekking with our remaining time. We're both tempted by this option, but it seems a waste to come all this way and not even try.

'This mountaineering's an expensive business,' I say to Mark. 'We've paid for all our permits, expedition insurance, and kit for a fully supported mountaineering expedition, and in the end, apart from that foray up to Camp 2, we've done no more than that Czech couple and Aussie trekker we saw. We could have saved ourselves a couple of grand.'

'I don't think they came over Sherpani Col and West Col,' Mark replies. 'I feel like we've done a bit more than your average trek.'

The sky continues to cloud over throughout the afternoon. Everybody huddles inside their tents. There's an eerie silence about the campsite, made all the more sinister by the flapping wings of *goraks* (ravens) overhead.

The forecasts are getting worse. At lunch Mark

reads out another that says there will be heavy snowfall at 7,200m and 65km per hour winds. This would basically wipe out the summit ridge.

Mark speculates again about abandoning the mountain altogether.

'If this forecast is correct then we might as well piss off now.'

'It'll feel a bit lame if we go home after just a stroll up to Camp 2,' I reply,

'It'll also feel a bit stupid going up there, in heavy snow, to sit in Camp 1 in a gale and come down again. I'm not up for that,' Mark says.

Throughout the afternoon, as I sit in our tent reading my book, I debate with myself what to do if a summit window is as hopeless as it seems. Meanwhile Mark watches two figures climbing towards the summit as clouds sail by overhead. This must be their last opportunity, but have the snow conditions stabilised enough?

Later that afternoon, we are sitting on the floor of the dining tent, drinking tea, when the door swings open and Dawa enters. He is followed into the tent by another climber, in his fifties with a furrowed expression on his face, and two other Sherpas. One of the Sherpas is a friend of Dawa's, and the climber is his leader, who has asked to be introduced to us.

I recognise the climber immediately. He is Sandy Allan, a well-known Scottish mountain guide. I climbed Gran Paradiso in Italy with him a few years ago as part of a commercial group, but it was such a long time ago that I'm certain he won't remember. It turns out that he is nominally our expedition leader here on Baruntse. In Nepal, climbing permits work out cheaper per person for larger teams. This encourages trekking agencies to group smaller teams together onto a single permit with one named leader. There are actually four small teams listed on our permit, and Sandy has been listed as our leader, even though he is only leading his own team.

I remember finding him a little gruff when I climbed with him in 2003, but on this occasion he's friendly and helpful, and gives us some useful advice. He tells us two Czech climbers reached the summit today, and three Sherpas yesterday. The Sherpas fixed ropes most of the way to the top. He says snow conditions have stabilised, and although snow is forecast tomorrow, the rest of the week is set to be fine.

While we're having this conversation, he's looking at both of us in a funny way.

'Do I know you guys from somewhere? You look familiar,' he finally says.

Mark admits to having climbed Mont Blanc with him several years ago, and afterwards he tells me he was keeping quiet for the same reason I was – that he had found Sandy somewhat difficult.

The old mountaineering seesaw continues to sway. From the doom and gloom of this afternoon there's no doubt that Sandy's optimistic outlook has offered us a ray of sunshine. We invite Dawa into the dining tent to talk things over. Although it's no more than a glimmer, all three of us agree that it might be better to push back our summit attempt to Tuesday, and climb up to Camp 1 on Monday. This will give tomorrow's snow more time to consolidate, and offers the possibility of more teams breaking trail to the summit in the meantime.

DAY 19
LOST CLIMBERS

Sunday, 31 October 2010 – Baruntse Base Camp, Nepal

There is light snow this morning, as the forecast predicted, and we feel justified in our decision to have another rest day here at base camp. I start a new book, *The Cruise of the Alerte* by E.F. Knight, a true 19th-century story of sailors looking for buried treasure on a desert island in the Atlantic Ocean. The back cover explains how the author lost his right arm yet continued to sail, quite literally single handed. His story makes sitting around at base camp feel less than heroic.

Nevertheless, as the forecast continues to be correct and the snow falls more heavily, it's an afternoon to stay in the tent reading. An inch or two of snow paints a white carpet over camp, and clouds sweep across Baruntse until nothing is visible beyond the far side of the lake. We hope not too much has fallen higher up the mountain, but by dinner six inches lie on the ground, and Dawa sidles into the dining tent for a discussion.

'What you think?' he says.

'What do *you* think?' Mark replies.

Dawa is always cagey about giving an opinion. He's been very flexible in allowing us to make our own decisions about our travelling itinerary. But when he's ventured an opinion, we've almost always followed his advice. Now that we've reached a critical stage his thoughts as an experienced mountain guide on his fifth expedition to Baruntse are more valuable than ever.

'Yes, what do you think, Dawa?' I repeat.

'I don't think…'

We wait for him to finish, but after a few seconds it becomes clear he's not going to add any more.

I start laughing.

'What do you mean, you don't think? You must think something.'

'I think it very difficult for us to continue on our own,' he says finally. 'Trail need breaking, and rope need digging out.'

'And presumably by tomorrow the fixed ropes will be frozen in?'

'Depend how much snow. A few foot, OK, maybe. Four or five foot – impossible.'

It's now clear that as a small team we don't have much hope, but we might have a chance with the cooperation of larger and better-resourced teams on the mountain. In other words, our own plans are dependent on theirs.

Chief among these teams is SummitClimb, who we

believe have 22 clients and umpteen Sherpas, including those who fixed the route to the summit two days ago. We contributed rope to this effort – they will be happy for us to use the lines they fixed.

But SummitClimb are running out of time, and are currently at Camp 2 before their summit attempt tomorrow. If they are successful, then not only will they have dug out the fixed ropes buried under fresh snow, but with such a large group they will have broken a good trail through thick snow, opening up the route again. On the other hand, if they decide there's too much snow to attempt the summit, and they descend, then both jobs will still need to be done.

Then there's the Adventure Peaks team, consisting of five clients, a leader and two Sherpas. They were on the same schedule as us, intending to go to Camp 1 today and attempt the summit tomorrow, until we considered the weather forecast and decided late last night to stay in base camp. Given the amount of snow that has fallen, we feel our decision has been vindicated – but they had the same forecast as we did, and they decided to press on.

It's getting late. We need to make a decision about tomorrow. Dawa says he will go to Adventure Peaks' base camp and talk to their Sherpas, who are in contact with the rest of their team in Camp 1, and find out what their plans are.

He returns only a few minutes later.

'That was quick,' Mark says.

'There is problem. Some of clients are missing.'

'Missing – where?'

'I assume between the top of West Col and Camp 1,' Mark says.

'But that's only a few metres,' I reply. 'All they need to do is keep the hill on their left and stumble into camp.'

But then I remember that Adventure Peaks have not put their Camp 1 underneath the small hill above West Col like everyone else, but out in the open on the way to Camp 2. This is several hundred metres further, across a featureless snow plateau, and if fresh snow has obliterated the tracks, then there is nothing to mark its position. I remember that nobody has put bamboo wands at regular intervals to mark the trail; the only wands we saw were marking crevasses.

This is a desperate situation. If their clients have overshot camp or set off in the wrong direction, they could be walking a long way across a featureless plateau – in the dark, possibly in a whiteout, in the cold, and with fresh snow quickly covering their footprints behind them.

Dawa switches on his radio so that we can listen to their conversation. Two Nepali voices are talking very quickly; then the voice of Adventure Peaks' leader cuts in.

'You could set off some fire crackers, or light a fire so that we can see you,' he says.

Light a fire? I think to myself. This seems wildly impractical. I look at the others; we're all thinking the same thing.

There is another crackle on the radio. Then: 'OK, I've got you, I see your light.'

Dawa goes outside, then shouts to us, 'OK, I see them, they are coming.'

We follow Dawa out. There on the other side of the lake is a party of dark figures approaching camp.

I laugh. 'I think that's what you call bathos.'

It's a relief, but something of an anticlimax. It turns out that the clients were not lost on the Barun Plateau, as we'd feared, but between the bottom of West Col and base camp. Conditions were so bad that instead of continuing to Camp 1 they have decided to come down again.

'I'm so glad we changed our minds at the last minute and stayed here today,' I remark. 'We're getting good at this.'

'What, sitting on our arses in base camp, looking at the weather forecast?'

'We seem to be making the right decisions.'

'That's 'cos between us we've got quite a bit of experience at sitting on our arses in shitty weather. It's all down to luck at the end of the day.'

'I'm just trying to think under what possible circumstances we might have gone to the summit yesterday, like those two Czech guys.'

'Well, we'd need to have known the route to the summit was getting fixed the previous day,' Mark says.

'But we couldn't have known that. In order to be in position the next day, we'd need to have been making our way up to Camp 2 while they were fixing.'

'Exactly – it's just luck. Being in the right place at the right time.'

'So if our whole expedition had been running two days later, we'd have been in position the other day when we went up to Camp 2, and we could have stayed there.' I throw my hands up in the air as I realise the futility of speculating. 'This is stupid – we can no more push the expedition back a couple of days than control the weather.'

'Unless you're the Chinese,' Mark says. 'They allegedly changed the weather around the Beijing Olympics to make it sunny for two weeks.'

I'm about to question this absurd suggestion, but then I remember he's a mine of useless trivia, and if I start another argument then I will probably lose.

'The only thing for certain is that we're in the hands of the mountain gods,' I reply.

'The mountain gods – are you sure?' Mark says.

We both start laughing, and I realise it's definitely time to end the conversation.

DAY 20
FROSTBITE

Monday, 1 November 2010 – Baruntse Base Camp, Nepal

It's still snowing when I peer out of the tent at 7am this morning, and it seems obvious that we won't be going anywhere again today.

'Have we given ourselves long enough?' I ask Mark. 'Did we need more spare days to climb this mountain?'

'I think we've given ourselves plenty of time,' he replies. 'I don't think anyone expected the weather to be this shit for so long. I mean, this much fresh snow one day after the ropes got fixed to the summit – that's just unlucky.'

Mark's right. It's the nature of mountaineering; you can do all the necessary preparation, but after that it's down to good fortune.

By 8.30am the sky has cleared completely, and we find ourselves in a winter wonderland. Our silver lake is surrounded by a lily-white carpet of deep snow, and Baruntse rises ever brighter on the opposite side.

But appearances are deceiving – this is not such a wonderland. Nobody yet knows the condition of the snow or the fixed ropes on the summit ridge, and whether the mountain has closed its gates. Then we hear the buzz of a helicopter overhead. From the door of the dining tent Mark sees a man walking towards us, propped up by a Sherpa.

'He's limping badly,' Mark says.

It's one of the Czechs who reached the summit two days ago. His companion is walking a little way behind him.

'My friend – his leg frozen,' he says as he passes our camp.

'So it wasn't much of a summit window after all,' I say to Mark once they've passed.

'That's great,' he replies, 'the only two people to make it to the summit, and one gets frostbite and has to be evacuated by helicopter.'

We know they reached the summit some time after midday. This means they would mostly have been climbing when the sun was up, although it was overcast that day. It must have been very cold indeed up there – it's debatable whether that day was a summit window at all. Is a summit worth frostbite? The answer has to be *no*. If you lose a digit each time then it's just ten summits before all your toes are gone. And the effects could be far worse than that.

It remains cold and sunny all day. It would be a most pleasant spot were we not contemplating the summit. We're reliant on other teams now. We think that SummitClimb have moved up to Camp 2 to put themselves in position for a summit bid tomorrow. With Adventure Peaks, it's less clear. All we know is that some of them are still up there – either at Camp 1 or Camp 2 – and haven't come down.

Other factors are less positive, too. None of the snow here at base camp has melted, despite the sun. This means that snow high on the mountain may be freezing into a hard, avalanche-prone surface crust. We think the winds up there are still 25km per hour, and there is no sign of them diminishing.

It's not the most positive scenario for a summit push, but we have no choice – tomorrow we must go for it. At least it will be good to be moving at long last, after four days at base camp.

DAY 21
DEFEATED

Tuesday, 2 November 2010 – Baruntse Base Camp, Nepal

One final swing of the seesaw. We learned late last night that SummitClimb won't be going for the summit today after all. They're still at Camp 1, after trying to get to Camp 2 yesterday in the thick snow, then retreating. This changes things for us. The trail to the summit won't be broken, and we'll all have to be on the summit ridge at the same time – one big, extremely slow group.

It was bitterly cold last night at base camp, a good five degrees colder than any previous night, and everything inside the tent is covered in a thick layer of frost this morning. We get dressed for our ascent in the freezing cold. The sun doesn't rise above the ridge to warm us until 8am. Only then does the temperature rise above -10°C.

Over breakfast Mark makes the decision to jump ship.

'A traffic jam on the summit ridge with

SummitClimb? I don't fancy that, even if anyone gets that high,' he says.

Then, as Dawa and I are getting ready to leave, we overhear a conversation on the radio between members of the Adventure Peaks group and a pair of French climbers at Camp 1. Almost all of them have decided to come down because they say that snow conditions are dangerous up there.

'There's been a lot of fresh snow. We're worried it might avalanche,' we overhear one of them saying.

One of the team leaders sounds like he is down in base camp, but he is being flexible with his clients and allowing them to make up their own minds about whether to continue. Dawa uses the same radio frequency to discuss the situation with some of his Sherpa colleagues in other teams. There are two conversations going on, but we all seem to be leaning towards the same conclusion. Everything is stacking up against us: waist-deep snow that's stopping everyone from getting to Camp 2, fixed ropes still buried under snow on the summit ridge, frostbite risk from freezing cold temperatures, a summit day stuck behind a huge group of climbers whose Sherpas we're relying on to help break trail. And now, most importantly of all, dangerous snow conditions that will require days to consolidate. Days we don't have.

'Is there a crust on top, with powder underneath,' I hear a voice say.

'Yeah, it's a bit like that.'

I turn to Dawa and shake my head. 'I've heard enough. These are exactly the conditions we had on

Cho Oyu... Two of the Sherpa rope teams triggered avalanches and were swept down the mountain. They were in a bad way.'

There are few things more likely to start an avalanche than 20 or 30 climbers tramping over unconsolidated snow at the same time. After much patience, it's time to concede defeat.

'Let's go,' I say.

Dawa looks surprised. 'Up?'

'No, down. Down and out. Let's get out of here.'

Now there is a look of disappointment on his face. Even after hearing this conversation over the radio, I can see that he still cherishes a hope of reaching the summit. He is a true climber, but he has to accept that Mark and I are not as bold.

Later this morning, Pasang takes some of the porters up to Camp 1 to retrieve the tents and our kit. Mark and I decide to have a leg stretch after four days of sitting around, so we wander for two hours up the moraine in the direction of West Col. After this morning's freezing temperatures, the sun is now beating down, and it's swelteringly hot. We stop at the foot of the glacier and spend half an hour contemplating Baruntse, but we have no regrets.

The wade through fresh snow has been tiring. How much more tiring to go all the way to the top in these conditions? Looking back, a sea of white lies before us all the way across the valley, and we can see the Amphu Labtsa, the difficult pass that we crossed last year.

It's a place to let the imagination run wild, but not

as much as Mark's does – he swears he sees four gnomes' faces in the snow face behind us. Try as I might I can't see them, but I take a photo to show to Mark after he's been drinking (i.e. his more usual state) to see if he can still see them then. Eventually we get cold and wander back down to base camp.

Mark Dickson on the route up to West Col, with Ama Dablam (6,814m) on the horizon behind

Throughout the afternoon, returning climbers – all at the end of their expeditions – pass us as we sit in our dining tent. We hear SummitClimb's Sherpas have succeeded in cutting a route up the short snow slope from Camp 1 to Camp 2, but I'd be surprised if there are any more summits on Baruntse this year, although some are still clinging on in hope.

Dawa, Pasang and the crew arrive back from

clearing Camp 1 at 6.30, a little after dark. It's been a long day for them. They arrive with the news that one of the tents we left at Camp 1 four days ago has been trashed by the strong winds. This is of little consequence now, but it may have been significant for our logistics had we decided to stay the night up there.

DAY 22
CONSOLATION

Wednesday, 3 November 2010 – Rato Ora, Hongu Valley, Nepal

It's another bitterly cold night, on the fringes of my sleeping bag's comfort zone. I guess it to be as low as -15° to -20°C inside the tent, which means it could be as low as -30°C outside.

We wait until the sun has appeared after eight o'clock before we pack up and leave the tent. Dawa is standing outside, looking up at Baruntse's summit ridge. He has a surprise for us.

'I see SummitClimb,' he says.

'Where?' I ask.

'On summit ridge. I see black dot. Fifteen, approaching summit.'

We look up. It's true. There are black dots on the ridge. They could just as easily be rocks from where we are standing, but I have no doubt they are climbers. Dawa has obviously been watching them and seen that they are making progress (rocks tend to be less mobile).

We weren't expecting this.

'Fuck me,' Mark says.

I don't know if this is simple amazement, or frustration that we're not up there with them.

'It's effing cold,' I say, a little more politely. 'We're 1,700m lower down here. It must be brass monkeys up there.'

Mark and I retire to the dining tent for breakfast, and discuss this development. To be so close to the summit so early in the morning means they must have been climbing through the night, but even if they set off at midnight this is impressive – especially if they've been breaking trail through thick snow, and digging out fixed ropes that were frozen a metre or two below the surface. It hardly seems credible, but the evidence of moving specks on the summit ridge is before our eyes. The eight Sherpas who are breaking trail will certainly have earned their summit bonus.

I've been in this situation a few times now. We came here to climb Baruntse, but conditions have meant that we've not really done much climbing. Had we ascended to Camp 1 yesterday, as we'd intended, then we might have chosen to attempt the summit as well. Three of those dots could have been Mark, Dawa and I.

At times like these it's impossible not to ask yourself 'what if?'

'If it was minus thirty down here last night, it must have been closer to minus forty up there,' I say to Mark, 'and that's without the wind chill.'

There's no doubt it's windy up there. We can see

spindrift coming off the mountain, and our weather forecast estimated winds of 25km per hour.

'I guess we all have different levels of risk. Minus fifty degrees might be a summit window for some, but not for me.'

'It wouldn't surprise me if there are a few cases of frostbite tomorrow,' Mark adds.

Mark appears to be more relaxed about it than I am. It's obvious that he has no regrets.

After breakfast, as our crew are tidying away camp, we sit on a bank of snow and look up at the summit. We take photographs with our big zoom-lens cameras, and view their screens to see the progress of the SummitClimb team in greater detail. Climbers seem to be emerging onto the summit plateau in ones and twos. I count around seven in total who reach the summit. An equal number appear to turn around, and we see them heading down beneath the second summit, still some way below the main one. Spindrift is billowing high into the air; conditions can't be pleasant. It's not surprising some of the climbers have chosen to turn back.

At eleven o'clock Sandy Allan's team walk past on their way up to Camp 1. We wish them luck – their chances now seem good – and we wish we could be joining them, but their flights out of Lukla are not till the 12th, while ours are on the 9th. They have three days longer than us, just enough time for a summit dash.

Dawa comes over and we discuss their prospects.

'We could still go up,' he says.

He seems keen, but no matter how many times we count the days left to us, and discuss which route to take back to Lukla, there just aren't enough of them. Even the superman Dawa eventually concedes this.

We have a Baruntse post-mortem and discuss if there was anything we could have done differently. Our first chance was going to be on Monday, but then the heavy snowfall on Sunday put paid to that idea, as it did for many other people.

Our next chance was only going to be possible by following larger teams with more Sherpa resources. When SummitClimb failed to get from Camp 1 to Camp 2 two days ago, that chance was gone too.

Our third chance would have meant going to the summit on the same day as them – today – and following in their wake. But when we heard about the potentially dangerous snow conditions, and knowing what the winds and temperature would be, we decided not to take that risk. The risk encompassed not only death by avalanche, but also amputation due to frostbite, neither of which we fancied.

Our fourth and final chance would have been to go a day after them. We might have done this had we gone up to Camp 2 today and gone for the summit tomorrow, but our weather forecast – which has been accurate so far – is forecasting more snow tomorrow.

Of course, we could have ignored all this information, taken our chances and gone up anyway. That appears to be Sandy's approach, but he is a more serious mountaineer than we are.[6] Perhaps the weather will be fine tomorrow and Sandy's team will summit as well. Good luck to them if they do, but it won't change anything for us.

Another observation provides some consolation. We don't know how many of the seven figures who reached the summit were Sherpas and how many were clients, but Dawa feels that most will be Sherpas breaking trail. So perhaps only two clients reached the summit. It would have been a tough summit day today, and Sherpas are made of a substance something like krypton, which few westerners can ever hope to match. Just because today turned out to be a summit day for Sherpas doesn't mean it would have been for lesser folk like us.

In any case, what's done is done – and we have the greater consolation today of trekking back through one of the loveliest valleys in the Himalayas, the Hongu Valley.

The crew take a long time to pack away, so we have lunch before departing from base camp at 1pm. The Hongu Valley is all the more picturesque today for its carpet of snow. We follow tracks in the snow in a narrow valley, enclosed by hillside and moraine, until it widens into the broad bogland where we

---

6 In 2012, Sandy and his climbing partner Rick Allen (a different Rick Allen to the one who played drums in the mullet-festooned 80s glam-metal group Def Leppard) made the first ascent of 8,125m Nanga Parbat in Pakistan via the 15km Mazeno Ridge. During the final summit push, the two men survived for five days without food and three without water.

camped last year. The blue and white of sky and snow contrasts with the brown and red of tufted grass and berberis.

We reach a silver lake surrounded by sandy beaches, and pause briefly at a herder's hut that offers pleasant camping and looks across the lake to the gentle snow slopes of Mera South. But when a dozen German trekkers approach, Sarki decides to continue down the valley. The rest of us chase after him.

Porter in the Hongu Valley

We pass through rhododendron-clad hillsides. We pass a lake with a large sandy beach, and wander through snow-laden Scottish moorland. We cross a wide, pebble-dashed plain formed by the Hongu River, we admire the white walls of Kali Himal and Baruntse across the valley behind us, and we look up at the black cliffs and icy summit of Chamlang thousands of metres above us. Finally we arrive at a grassy platform in a narrow cutting beneath red cliff faces, and we stop to camp for the night with the sound of the river crashing beneath us.

The Hongu Valley is an amazing place, with such diversity to be seen in a short, four-hour walk from Baruntse Base Camp. And today's cloud cover meant that we didn't even get to see the massive black wall of Lhotse beyond the top end of the valley.

It's five o'clock and getting cold by the time we reach camp. Sarki calls the place Rato Ora, which translates as 'red cliff'. Mark and I make ourselves comfortable in our tent, and they bring us tea and biscuits, followed by dal bhat for dinner. We're at 4,900m now; although we are only 500m below base camp, we look forward to a night of more normal temperatures.

DAY 23
MERA SOUTH

Thursday, 4 November 2010 – Khare, Mera Peak trail, Nepal

After three weeks of remote passes and valleys, we hit the tourist trail today when we cross over the Mera La and meet up with all the trekkers and climbers on their way to Mera Peak. But this is a small price to pay. The scenery is lovely – and all the better because last year we came this way in thick mist and missed out on many of the views.

We leave camp at nine o'clock and have a stiff climb up to the point where we leave the Hongu Valley and pass into a side valley beneath the Mera La. We're high above the valley floor on pleasant grassy hillsides still laden with snow. Here a small turquoise lake nestles in a natural bowl; I remember it well from last year. Behind us, the huge bulk of Chamlang rises high above in a massive wall of snow and rock, by far the most dominant feature in this beautiful landscape.

Today my attention is directed towards the view of

Mera Peak in front of us. I'm not studying the two higher summits of Mera North and Mera Central that we climbed last year, but the lesser peak of Mera South, rising less prominently at the end of a jagged ridge to their left. This mountain attracted my attention several times yesterday, yet I hadn't noticed it when we passed this way before. I discussed it as an objective with Mark yesterday, and I decide to ask Dawa about it today.

'We climbed North and Central last year, so it seems only fair that we complete the set by climbing Mera South as well,' I say.

'You want climb it now? Very easy, but very many crevasse.'

I hadn't been thinking of climbing it now, but we have a spare day, and Dawa has planted the seed of an idea that has blossomed into intent by the time we reach last year's campsite at Kongme Dingma 20 minutes later.

'So how about a consolation prize?' I ask Mark. 'Mera South.'

Dawa says there is an office of the Nepal Mountaineering Association (NMA) in Khare where we can get permits. Khare is the other side of the Mera La; we would need to cross the pass, then come back again to climb the mountain. We fish Mark's satellite phone out of his kit bag and spend about 45 minutes at Kongme Dingma trying to get in touch, to see if we can climb Mera South first, then buy the permit retrospectively on our way through Khare. This would prevent us having to cross the Mera La twice, and save us several hours in a tight schedule.

Dawa gets through to the office. They tell him we can't – but Mera South is still possible if we are prepared to make up the time with longer days on the trek back to Lukla.

Looking across a lake to Mera South (left),
with Mera Peak's main summits on the right

We climb slowly up the hillside above Kongme Dingma on grassy slopes, slippery with compacted snow. The view behind us up at Chamlang is breathtaking. After about 300m of ascent we crest a rise marked by a cairn and prayer flags. Here we can see all the Meras lined up in a single panorama, from Mera South on the left, along a jagged ridge to the much higher snowfield and snow domes of Meras Central and North.

We're now tantalisingly close to Mera South. It's heavily crevassed, so much so that we can't see an obvious route through the maze. It reminds me of Antisana in Ecuador, which I climbed last December, and also found to be riddled with crevasses.[7] This made for some interesting climbing. But on Antisana our guides had spoken to people who had climbed it a few days earlier, and they already had a good idea of the route. There was a certain amount of route-finding on the day, but it didn't delay us too significantly.

On Mera South we would need to find a route ourselves.

'Not possible,' says Dawa. 'May take two or three day to find route.'

Sadly, we only have time for one desperate summit dash. Mera South has proved to be a far more interesting proposition than we first envisaged; unfortunately it's not one we can tackle now.

We turn our attention to the right of the panorama and continue up to the Mera La, crossing a black sandy plateau, and ascend a scree slope to the pass. A handful of tea shops mark the Mera La campsite: a place where I've spent one or two bleak afternoons in the past. This time the sun is out. We enjoy a clear view of the route all the way up to the summit of Mera Central.

The pass itself is spanned by the Mera Glacier, which climbs in a continuous sweep of snow and ice

---

7 See my book *Feet and Wheels to Chimborazo*.

all the way to the summit. In order to cross the pass we have to put on crampons and walk to the right, down the glacier's lower reaches. It's been a flat expanse of ice when I've been here before, but this year it's riddled with yawning crevasses that make it very picturesque.

The snout of the glacier also stands in marked contrast to its state last year, when it was necessary to climb steeply down frozen pinnacles of rock-hard ice in order to reach dry land again. This year there's been so much snow that the same descent has become a straightforward (albeit steep) snow slope.

It's not so straightforward for Pasang, who is walking in front of me. He descends tentatively, armed with just walking boots and stick on a slope that I'm taking carefully with axe and crampons. When he reaches the bottom safely, he tells me it's been good practice for him. On his basic mountaineering course, they taught him how to climb steep snow slopes without crampons – a skill we don't learn at home.

From the snout of the glacier it's an easy descent of 500m on rocky slopes to the relative metropolis of Khare, the first substantial village we've passed through in weeks. There are several trekking groups camped here on their Mera Peak expeditions. We choose to camp on the back terrace of a teahouse we believe to be empty, but when I walk up to the dining room, I find it packed with French trekkers. From their things spread out all over the tables I deduce that they're sleeping there. When I ask for a bit of table room to sit at, they refuse to budge.

We retire to our tent to unpack, full of mischievous ideas. Mark suggests buying our porters *chang* (rice beer), to encourage them to stay up partying, and keep the trekkers awake. But when we go to dinner at seven o'clock, the group has had a change of heart. Most have retired to bedrooms and tidied away a table in the dining room for us to eat at. Those who remain are polite and friendly, and Anglo-French relations are restored. We pass an enjoyable dinner chatting to Dawa about mountains and mountaineering.

DAY 24
HOT LUNCH FRUSTRATION

Friday, 5 November 2010 – Kote, Mera Peak trail, Nepal

Today finds me strangely irritable about minor things. It starts with our morning wake-up, when the crew provide breakfast before we've finished packing up our kit, so that the food goes cold. Then they start dismantling the tent while we're still in it. I approve of packing up and getting ready with speed, but only when they give us due notice. We agreed breakfast at the relatively late hour of 8.30, and here they are dismantling the tent at 8am.

On average, it's taken us two to three hours to get away each morning. This is a stupidly long time, but we haven't complained, because we assumed our shortage of porters was the reason. Now we're getting close to the end of the expedition and we're still short of porters, but they seem perfectly able to break camp quickly. So why were they taking so long before?

We get away at ten o'clock. Pasang leads us quickly out of Khare and down the steep river valley towards Tangnag – so quickly, in fact, that whenever I stop for a photo I have to run to catch up. The trail is busy with trekking groups and porters on the way up to Mera Peak. It's another picturesque section of trail: the river falls rapidly over rocky cascades as the path winds alongside, and the twin-domed trekking peak of Kusum Kangguru rises overhead. We pass briefly through a wide sandy area before the river plunges across boulders to the village of Tangnag at the head of the Hinku Valley.

Descending towards Tangnag with
Kusum Kanguru and Kyashar up ahead

It's been a rapid descent. At 11.30 we reach the village, which consists of a few trekkers' lodges and adjoining campsites in a broad, flat area at a junction of valleys. The steep flank of Mera Peak rises like a wall on one side, but the adjoining valleys provide more distant views and a feeling of space. It's a place that provides fond memories. I stayed here in 2004 after a large group of us had climbed Mera, and enjoyed an evening of celebration with our crew. After they sang us a local Nepali tune, we were asked to sing a British song in return. We ended up doing an *a cappella* version of Bohemian Rhapsody, complete with headbanging and air guitars. The following morning, I overheard someone from another group complaining that they were kept awake by people shouting 'scaramouche, scaramouche' in a nearby teahouse.

This time I don't feel quite as joyful. Pasang tells us that we'll be having lunch here, and my heart sinks – we've barely been walking for an hour, and now we face another long wait for food that I know won't be very palatable.

I get out my journal, lean against a wall and begin to write. Meanwhile Mark lies down on the grass and falls asleep. An hour and a half later there's still no sign of lunch, so I go for a wander around the village. There isn't much to see. When I arrive back ten minutes later I decide to walk up one of the hillsides overlooking the village. I've walked for about ten minutes when I hear people whistling down below and calling my name – lunch at last. I'm in a petulant mood now, so I ignore them and walk for a little longer. I sit down on the grass for a few minutes to admire the view, then amble back down again. I arrive back at the tea shop they've chosen to eat in, aware that I've delayed lunch by about 15 minutes, but I am feeling slightly rebellious and I do not apologise.

I try to think which element of the hot lunches we've had so far that I might look forward to the most, and I come up with cheese. By happy chance today's lunch is one of the few that includes cheese. My plate also contains a handful of fried chips, which I eat with equal relish, as well as a couple of stodgy vegetable dishes, which I leave.

I feel a twinge of guilt for making a scene, but the long delays for hot lunch are becoming farcical. We're wasting the best part of the day, sitting around waiting to eat not very palatable food, instead of doing what we're here to do – enjoy the walking in a beautiful landscape. By the time we arrive in camp this afternoon it will be late, and we will have walked the last hour in shade because the sun has gone down behind the mountains. It will be much colder, and the absence of sunlight will make my photographs a little dull.

I ask Dawa if we can have packed lunches for the remaining two days. Three hot meals a day are unnecessary; both Mark and I are quite happy just snacking on chocolate. Dawa is our sirdar, and technically in charge, but Sarki is the cook, and cooks have a special power I can't quite grasp. Dawa says he will ask.

We finally leave Tangnag at 2.30, three hours after we arrived. I remember the walk down the Hinku Valley from Tangnag to Kote as a pleasant one, passing through picturesque rhododendron-clad yak meadows, before descending along the valley floor on a less agreeable trail beside a rocky river bed. Only last year we spent a large part of the day passing through these meadows, but now erosion has changed the trail completely. The meadows are gradually falling into the river. The path has been diverted beneath them, and we spend almost all of this section boulder hopping along the river bed.

We reach Kote at 4.30: a village of timber shacks and trekking lodges on wooden platforms, with large, terraced camping grounds built up beside the river bed. Pine forests rise steeply up the mountainside above the village. The fast-flowing river crashes noisily past. Dawa finds us a private camping ground at the far end of the village, with our own little hut to eat in. A raised grassy terrace enables us to look out and survey the rest of the village and all the other trekking groups camping below us.

The hut is warm and cosy thanks to a fire burning in one corner. As soon as we've unpacked our kit in the tent, we settle down and enjoy a few San Miguel beers beside the fire. It's a pleasant end to the day, and by the time I return to the tent I am feeling much more relaxed.

DAY 25
THE WORLD'S MOST DANGEROUS TOILET ENTRANCE

Saturday, 6 November 2010 – Thuli Kharka, Hinku Valley, Nepal

We're back to the early starts again this morning with a 6am wake-up. Kote stands at around 3,600m in altitude, and it's noticeably warmer this morning: 5°C when we wake up, sheer pleasure compared with the sub -10°C temperatures we've experienced for most of the last two weeks.

From our lofty terrace, I watch all the other trekking groups packing away around the village. We leave at 8am. Kote sits on the fringes of the forest zone, and we begin by ascending slightly into forest of blue pine and rhododendron, before dropping about 200m back down to the river. From then on it's up, up, up for the rest of the day. We rise steadily through the forest on a broad pathway winding left and right around the hillside before climbing past lonely teahouses to reach a gully. A waterfall cascades over mossy rocks, and we climb steeply alongside it to a place called Taktha, where we stop for lunch. It's 11am; although I asked for packed lunches today, it looks like they have ignored my request. We brace ourselves for another long delay.

Across the river from our teahouse we watch a KE Adventure group have their lunch on a patch of grass beside a hut. Their kitchen crew have already been there for some time preparing the food. I look on enviously – their lunch is served as soon as they arrive, and they depart again within the hour.

Meanwhile Mark and I, who arrived before them, keep waiting. I buy myself a tube of Pringles and a Snickers bar from the teahouse, as I don't have high hopes for a palatable lunch. When it finally arrives, I stare at it for a couple of minutes before I can summon up the courage to bite into it. A dollop of baked beans, some undercooked curried potatoes, a splodge of boiled green beans, and a wedge of soggy pancake. I have about two mouthfuls of the baked beans before pushing the plate away.

Later, Mark tells me, 'Your face when lunch arrived was fucking hilarious.'

Afterwards I brave the toilet behind the teahouse: a wooden shack with a deep pit dug underneath. The entrance appears to be around the back, where a large rock angles steeply downwards in front of the open side of the shack, before dropping some 6m into the 'shit pit'. In order to reach the floor of the toilet I have to grab a wooden beam for security and leap from solid ground, over the sloping rock, and onto the raised platform of the toilet. To land on the rock would mean sliding down into the pit. Although it would be a soft landing, it's not an attractive prospect, and I would probably have to burn my clothes afterwards.

After surviving the ordeal, I describe the setting to Mark and warn him that it's one of the most dangerous toilet entrances in the world. Undeterred, he sets off, and returns a few minutes later with a puzzled look on his face.

'Instead of jumping over the gap at the back, why didn't you just go in through the door at the front?'

We leave our lunch stop at 1.30, just two and a half hours after arriving this time. The path continues to climb steeply, but the forest has thinned: gone are the blue pines and large rhododendron trees. Dwarf rhododendron bushes now span the pathway, gradually getting smaller as we ascend, until they disappear completely.

After 400m of ascent I reach a grassy spur where Mark and Pasang are waiting, having climbed more quickly than me. We have fine views up, down and across the Hinku Valley, and I remember this precise spot from when I climbed Mera Peak six years ago. Hillsides rise steeply 2,000m above the Hinku River, where we started this morning. A seemingly impossible pathway weaves its way around the hillside directly opposite us. This is the path I followed on both of my previous expeditions to Mera Peak; it's possible to trace all the places we visited along the way. To the left, rising above these dark hillsides, is Mera itself, a crown of three summits resting atop its sheer 2,000m south face. It's hard to believe there's a straightforward way up around the other side. Dawa, Mark and I traversed this path to Mera last year, and it's interesting to see the terrain we passed through from this angle.

Looking across the Hinku Valley to Mera Peak
from the ascent to the Zatr La

After a short break we continue on our way. The sky has clouded over now, and the scene changes again. A narrow path weaves up and down a cliff face before cresting a spur marked by prayer flags. Beyond this it drops into grassy moorland encrusted with boulders – a little taste of Scotland hidden away on this high plateau among steep valleys.

We round a corner and climb gently to half a dozen

teahouses nestling within this moorland scene. We arrive at the village of Thuli Kharka in a light mist. The village is situated at 4,250m in altitude, just 300m below the Zatr La, the gateway to Lukla. It's 3.30 when we arrive. We must be some way ahead of the porters, so we decide to take a room in one of the teahouses instead of camping, enabling us to warm ourselves up while we wait for our bags. We've sweated a lot during the climb and are glad of the dry clothes that we've been carrying in our packs.

For dinner, we have the toughest fried chicken I've eaten in my life. Unlike the 19th-century explorer John Franklin, I've never been so hungry that I've had to eat the leather of my boots, but I imagine they would have a similar consistency. I find it difficult to cut, so I pick the whole thing up and bite out a chunk. This is a mistake. I'm now eating a mouthful so large that I chew and chew and chew and nothing seems to happen. After about five minutes I've digested enough off the sides to be able to swallow the rest – but, like eating celery and lettuce, I've probably expended more energy chewing than the food has provided. Sawing it into bite-sized chunks is the only sensible angle of attack. It actually tastes quite nice, so I persevere until it's finished.

DAY 26
OVER THE ZATR LA

Sunday, 7 November 2010 – Lukla, Solu-Khumbu, Nepal

The sun is shining brightly when we leave Thuli Kharka at 8am. A light haze makes the mountains beneath us in the Hinku Valley appear as faint outlines disappearing towards the horizon. An enormous boulder 20 to 30m high rises like a tower block at the top end of the village. It is perched on its end and leaning slightly. I presume that it's been there a long time, but it would make me nervous if I lived in one of the houses beneath it. I'm glad I didn't see it when we arrived yesterday afternoon.

Today is the last day of our trek; we will cross the Zatr La, then descend to Lukla, the village with an airstrip that is the gateway to the Everest region. We climb nearly 400m over rolling moorland studded with grey granite boulders. It's easy walking in bright sunshine. We take it gently, stopping to look back and admire the view behind us that becomes broader the higher we climb. The Zatr La consists of two passes.

We reach the higher one at 9am, and a new vista greets us down into the Dudh Khosi Valley. This is a much more civilised valley than the Hinku, lined with villages and teahouses catering for trekkers on the Everest Base Camp trail. But up here at 4,610m, it still feels wild and remote.

On the other side of the pass, we have a short walk on one of those magnificent trails, so typical in Nepal, that traverses high across a mountainside. At the far end of it, we reach the second pass at 9.30 and stop for a short rest. We're now looking into the Khumbu region of Nepal; the airstrip at Lukla is 1,700m below us. A line of snow peaks stretches across the horizon ahead, culminating in 8,201m Cho Oyu, where I began my Himalayan journey on the Tibetan side back in August.

Porters traversing from the higher to the lower Zatr La

As we rest beneath fluttering pray flags, Dawa chooses this moment to talk about global warming.

'I think not snow much here any more,' he says, surveying the snow line on the peaks beyond us.

Given what's just happened to us on Baruntse, and my experience on Cho Oyu a few weeks earlier, Mark and I don't entirely agree with this statement.

'We have a phrase for that in the UK,' Mark says. "Bollocks".'

'I spent a month on that mountain over there earlier this year,' I say, 'and I can tell you there was plenty of snow up there.'

But Dawa is smiling, and he takes no offence at our reaction.

Last time I crossed the Zatr La in 2004 the weather was cloudy, we couldn't see far, and there was lots of snow on the Lukla side of the pass. We descended for 1,000m, sliding on our backsides at regular intervals: a painstaking and frustrating descent that seemed to go on and on. One of our group slipped and tripped over a porter, who promptly dropped his load to save himself. I remember watching a pair of blue duffle bags go flying past me down a narrow gully to my left, and continuing for a few hundred metres before coming to rest. Later I snapped one my trekking poles trying to arrest another slide.

Today the going is much easier, with clear views down into the Dudh Khosi Valley far below, but much of the west side of the pass seems to exist in permanent shade. In these areas, thousands of pairs of tramping feet have packed patches of snow down solid. We slide and slip on these treacherous glazed steps. Other than this, the biggest hazard is knee-ache as the path continues down and down past dark rocks, and through an extensive area of small rhododendron trees.

After 1,000m of descent we stop for lunch on grass terraces outside some tea shops. Mark and I treat ourselves to some 350-rupee tins of San Miguel beer.

'These are London night club prices,' I complain.

'I don't care. I'm buying them. I'll have yours if it's too expensive for you,' Mark replies.

The descent is more gradual after lunch as the path eases round a series of hillsides through rhododendron and bamboo. At 3.30 we reach Lukla, perched on a flattish platform big enough for an airstrip, high above the Dudh Khosi Valley. The village is a metropolis after our month in the wilderness. Beyond the airport a sprawling main street is packed with teahouses, trekking shops, bars and internet cafés.

We check in to the North Face Lodge at the end of the main shopping area. I've stayed in this teahouse many times before, and each time it seems to be a bit posher. Today we are given a big double room in an annex at the bottom of a landscaped garden. The room is without a number; all of the rooms in our annex are known by the names of mountains. Ours is called *Ama Dablam*, and we're delighted to discover that it has an en suite bathroom with hot shower, a real luxury after all this time without a proper wash. It also has paper-thin walls. I don't think the two

American women next door in *Everest*, who are screaming 'Ooh, ooh, there must be hot showers in heaven...', realise they are entertaining the rest of the annex.

Before long we're clean, in fresh clothes and looking for bars on the main street. We're tempted by one called Altitude advertising 'Happy Hour Buy Two Beers Get One Free', but we turn around when we hear Boney M's *Brown Girl in the Ring* blaring out from inside. Instead we choose the Irish Pub, down some stairs and through a low door. We both crack our heads as we enter. Here we have a game of pool with a German and a Pole who are so incompetent that we win one game before they've potted any balls. And I thought *I* was crap at pool.

We return to the North Face for dinner. Two huge trekking groups of 20 people or more, mostly elderly pensioners, are having their end-of-trek meals. One is French and the other Danish, and they end up having an impromptu sing-off. Each group tries to draw attention to itself by singing national songs louder than the other. After about 15 minutes the French seem to be winning hands down. The Danes are sitting around in silence, looking glum. They are rescued by their Sherpas, who leap up and start dancing when some Nepali music comes on. The Danish oldies jump to their feet in response and the game swings back in their favour.

But the French are not to be outdone. They also get up and start leaping around. Suddenly we're in a crowded restaurant, with painted Buddhas on the ceiling, full of old people jumping up and down to Nepali music. The floor boards are shaking. It's one of the most ridiculous things I've ever seen in my life.

'Let's get out of here,' I say to Mark.

'I think it's time,' he replies.

We find our crew eating dal bhat in a dark and dingy hut adjoining the lodge. We've promised to buy them alcohol, and the restaurant of the North Face Lodge is considered too upmarket for them (although the scene being played out upstairs would seem to belie this).

Sarki finds a little Nepali locals' bar down the road, which is much more conducive to what Mark has planned – drinking games. He teaches our crew a favourite of his called the 'Hand Game'. This involves everyone sitting around a table and putting the palms of both hands face down on its surface. We then go round in a ring, tapping each hand on the table in sequence. A single tap advances the tapping in the same direction, a double tap skips a hand, and a triple tap reverses the direction. To make things harder, we have to weave our arms together so that our hands are crossed with the people on either side of us. If anyone makes a mistake then they have to drink *rakshi* – the local Nepali home-made firewater.

It's a game that transcends language. For some two hours I sit with my arms spread apart on the table, with Dawa's right hand and Karma's left one on the table in front of me. Every so often someone misses a tap; all the porters cry 'rakshi penalty' in unison, and we collapse into hoots of raucous laughter. We eventually leave at midnight. Someone has locked the gate in to our posh annex of the North Face, and Mark and I have to leap over a barbed-wire fence to get back in. We assume the French and the Danes are exhausted by then and sleeping soundly.

It's an entertaining conclusion to what has sometimes been a frustrating and disappointing expedition. It's at times like these that I have to pinch myself hard, and remind myself how lucky I am to be travelling through such beautiful scenery, with such cheerful people. We wanted to climb a mountain, but instead we spent five days camping at its base. This is only a disappointment if we consider the climb to be the primary focus of our trip. If instead we consider it to be the icing on a delicious cake of Himalayan trekking, then our trip has been a mouth-watering feast.

It may not have gone our way this time, but we'll be back for sure.

EPILOGUE

Base camps on busy mountains are not a good place to find reliable information. They are alive with rumour. Climbers and expedition staff share gossip, and plans change from hour to hour with every change in the weather. Information is often shared second or third hand, changing as it passes from person to person like a game of Chinese whispers.[8] With satellite technology, sometimes people will share rumours online and then not bother to correct them when things become clearer, so that misinformation remains in the ether.

Luckily, in Nepal there is one source that can be considered reliable. In the 1960s, an American journalist called Elizabeth Hawley moved to Kathmandu and began interviewing climbers about their expeditions on behalf of Reuters, the news agency she was working for at the time. She continued to do this for the rest of her life, eventually interviewing every team attempting a peak over 7,000m. In the 1990s her records began to be digitised,

---

8 See my book *Thieves, Liars and Mountaineers* for an extreme example of this phenomenon in action.

and in 2004 the Himalayan Database was first published. Since her death in 2018, the work has continued under the leadership of German journalist Billi Bierling.

The information in the Himalayan Database isn't perfect. It is only one person's opinion – the team leader's. In our case that was Sandy Allan, who was listed as leader on our climbing permit. Neither Mark nor I were interviewed; consequently, there is no information about our expedition in the Himalayan Database, other than the fact that it took place and we didn't reach the summit.

Thanks to the database, however, I was able to learn that after passing us on 3 November, Sandy and his team went up to Camp 2, and left for the summit at 2am on 5 November. Sandy, two clients and three Sherpas all reached the summit by 9.30am and reported that it was windy on top, but calm down below. The skies were clear, and although the temperature wasn't mentioned in their report, I expect it was very cold. I also learned that all eight clients and eight Sherpas from the SummitClimb team reached the summit between 10am and 12 noon on 3 November, which just goes to show that not everything is what it seems – this isn't what we thought we saw from down below. There was no mention in their report of anyone turning around.

And what happened to Chewang Nima? When accidents like this take place in the mountains of Nepal, the team from the Himalayan Database are always diligent about discovering and reporting the details. He had been hired by an experienced, 27-year-old American mountain guide called Melissa Arnot, who had already climbed Everest three times. They planned to do a fast ascent, and climbed directly from Base Camp to Camp 2 on 22 October, the day that Mark and I left Makalu Base Camp on the eastern side of Baruntse.

The following day, 23 October, when Mark injured his knee putting his leg in a gap between boulders on the way up to Sherpani Col, a far more tragic event was unfolding on Baruntse. Chewang Nima and Nima Gyalzen, a Sherpa with an Iranian team, set out from Camp 2 at 10.30am to break trail and fix ropes to the summit. They stayed out all day, and by 3.30 they had climbed just above 7,000m on the summit ridge when they encountered a crevasse with a cornice on its north-west side.

A cornice is a ledge of snow overhanging a drop. They are not always easy to spot; but every experienced mountaineer knows to keep well clear of the edge of one, and be sure they have solid ground beneath their feet. Perhaps the two Sherpas didn't realise it was a cornice until it was too late. Or perhaps they believed that because they were roped together, they would be able to hold each other if one of them fell through. Whatever the reason, Chewang Nima decided to climb on top, and was banging a picket into the snow when the cornice collapsed, plunging him over Baruntse's east face, and sending an avalanche of fluted snow and rock behind him. Nima Gyalzen only survived because the collapsing ice sliced the rope between them and severed it.

Melissa was making tea when he arrived back at Camp 2 at 5pm.

'Chewang finished,' he cried.

They descended to Base Camp in darkness, and the next morning they called a helicopter to look for Chewang Nima. But strong winds on Baruntse's east side meant that a search wasn't possible that day, so instead they flew to Chewang's village to visit his family and report the tragedy.

On 25 October, Mark and I made our first acclimatisation hike up to Sherpani Col. Had we listened closely, we might have heard the sound of a helicopter flying across the ridge to our north. Melissa and Nima had trekked to Namche, where the Italian climber and helicopter pilot Simone Moro picked them up to fly them to Kharikhola, a village on the Jiri-to-Lukla trail. Here they picked up Chewang's brother, Nima Nuru and flew to a hilltop near Baruntse to conduct another search for any sign of Chewang Nima. They looked for nearly an hour. But they could see there had been three huge avalanches which meant there was virtually no chance of finding him.

Chewang Nima Sherpa was born in 1967 and lived in the village of Tesho, near Thame in the Khumbu region of Nepal. His mountaineering career came to be dominated by Everest. It was widely reported that he climbed it 19 times, though the Himalayan Database lists only 18 ascents. He first climbed it in 1994 on a commercial expedition with the American operator Alpine Ascents. He eventually became a regular with Alpine Ascents, climbing Everest nine times with them, including twice on his last expedition in 2010 (when he helped to fix ropes to the summit on 5 May, then returned there with clients on 24 May). He also joined Japanese, Indonesian and Australian expeditions. Five of his ascents were from the north side of the mountain. He also climbed it twice in the autumn season, from both the south side (with a Japanese team in 1994) and on the north side (with an Indonesian team in 1996, when he helped Clara Sumarwati to become the first Indonesian woman and first Indonesian to reach the summit of Everest).

The Himalayan Database lists him only five more times – for two ascents of Cho Oyu, two ascents of Ama Dablam, and his final expedition to Baruntse. His 17 Everest expeditions and 18 ascents made him the legend that he is.

ACKNOWLEDGEMENTS

Thanks to Mark Dickson for being entertaining company on this and many other expeditions to the Himalayas over the years.

Big thanks to our kitchen crew: Sarki the cook, Pasang the assistant cook, and kitchen assistants Karma and Mingma. We were indebted to our huge band of some 30 cheerful porters, five of whom crossed the high passes and came with us all the way to Lukla.

Thanks to Dawa Bhote for being a safe and reliable climbing guide, to Pasang the guide, and to Siling Ghale and Tina Stacey of The Responsible Travellers for their assistance with trip planning.

Thanks to my editor, Alex Roddie, for his help polishing the text.

Most of all thanks to all of you, readers of my blog and diaries. I hope you have enjoyed this one, and I look forward to welcoming you back sometime. If you have not read them already then I hope you will enjoy my other books, which you can find listed on my website at www.markhorrell.com/books.

ISLANDS IN THE SNOW

A journey to explore Nepal's trekking peaks

Two days east of Lukla was a pleasant yak pasture surrounded by high peaks. When Col. Jim Roberts set out to look for it in 1953, he ended up making the first ascent of Mera Peak and sowing the seeds of Himalayan tourism.

Mera Peak has become a popular goal for trekkers and novice mountaineers, but few people climb to its true summit, and fewer still travel beyond it to find the secret yak pasture that sparked Roberts' journey.

The yak pasture was the Hongu Valley, a hidden sanctuary of grassland, lakes and glaciers linking Mera Peak with the Everest region and Island Peak to the north. Fifty years after Roberts, Mark Horrell embarked on a trek through Nepal's Khumbu region to follow in his footsteps, climb the two trekking peaks at either end of the valley, and resolve a long-standing mystery about Mera Peak's height.

Join Mark on a captivating journey through this enchanting region of high mountains and remote valleys.

Published in 2018. A list of bookstores can be found on Mark's website:

www.markhorrell.com/Islands

SEVEN STEPS FROM SNOWDON TO EVEREST

A hill walker's journey to the top of the world

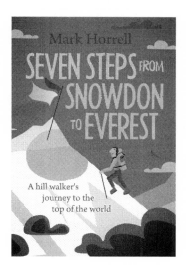

As he teetered on a narrow rock ledge a yak's bellow short of the stratosphere, with a rubber mask strapped to his face, a pair of mittens the size of a sealion's flippers, and a drop of two kilometres below him, it's fair to say Mark Horrell wasn't entirely happy with the situation he found himself in.

He was an ordinary hiker who had only read books about mountaineering, and little did he know when he signed up for an organised trek in Nepal with a group of elderly ladies that ten years later he would be attempting to climb the world's highest mountain.

But as he travelled across the Himalayas, Andes, Alps and East Africa, following in the footsteps of the pioneers, he dreamed up a seven-point plan to gain the skills and experience which could turn a wild idea into reality.

Funny, incisive and heartfelt, his journey provides a refreshingly honest portrait of the joys and torments of a modern-day Everest climber.

First published in 2015. A list of bookstores can be found on Mark's website:

www.markhorrell.com/SnowdonToEverest

FEET AND WHEELS TO CHIMBORAZO

A unique climbing and cycling adventure to the summit of Ecuador

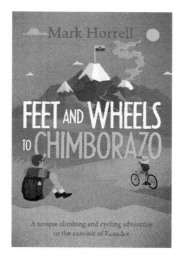

His cheeks are as tender as raw meat on a butcher's block. And those are just the cheeks of his face. As he slumps in the saddle, watching the road disappear into the distance, he aches in parts of his body that he's only just discovering he has…

When Mark travels to Ecuador to go hiking and climbing, he discovers a land of dramatic volcanoes rising through the clouds and wide-open horizons rich in history.

But when his partner Edita suggests a return visit, she has a very different adventure in mind: to cycle across the Andes and complete a unique sea-to-summit challenge by climbing the highest mountain starting from sea level.

It will be an intrepid world first (or so they think). But there's just one problem – Mark can barely cycle over a road bridge without getting off to push.

With a month to train, they rent some bikes and head to Scotland to cycle the North Coast 500. Will this be enough to prepare them for an epic adventure to climb a mountain that in one respect is the highest in the world?

First published in 2019. A list of bookstores can be found on Mark's website:

www.markhorrell.com/Chimborazo

PHOTOGRAPHS

I hope you enjoyed the photos in this book. Thanks to the miracles of the internet you can view all the photos from my Baruntse expedition online via the photo-sharing website *Flickr*.

Baruntse. Nepal, October/November, 2010:
www.markhorrell.com/Baruntse

ABOUT THE AUTHOR

For many years Mark Horrell has been writing what has been described as one of the most credible Everest opinion blogs out there. He writes about trekking and mountaineering from the often silent perspective of the commercial client.

For nearly 20 years he has been exploring the world's greater mountain ranges and keeping a diary of his travels. As a writer he strives to do for mountain history what Bill Bryson did for long-distance hiking.

Several of his expedition diaries are available from the major online bookstores. He has published two full-length books: *Seven Steps from Snowdon to Everest* (2015), about his ten-year journey from hill walker to Everest climber, and *Feet and Wheels to Chimborazo* (2019), about an expedition to cycle and climb from sea level to the furthest point from the centre of the earth.

His favourite mountaineering book is *The Ascent of Rum Doodle* by W.E. Bowman.

ABOUT THIS SERIES

The *Footsteps on the Mountain Diaries* are Mark's expedition journals. They are edited versions of what he scribbles in his tent each evening after a day in the mountains, with a bit of history thrown in. Light-hearted and engaging, they provide a perfect introduction to life on the trail.

For other titles in this series see Mark's website: www.markhorrell.com/diaries

CONNECT

You can join Mark's **mailing list** to keep updated:
www.markhorrell.com/mailinglist

Website and blog: www.markhorrell.com
Twitter: @markhorrell
Facebook:
www.facebook.com/footstepsonthemountain
Flickr: www.flickr.com/markhorrell
YouTube: www.youtube.com/markhorrell

DID YOU ENJOY THIS BOOK?

Thank you for buying and reading this book. Word-of-mouth is crucial for any author to be successful. If you enjoyed it then please consider leaving a review. Even if it's only a couple of sentences, it would be a great help and will be appreciated enormously.

Links to this book on the main online book stores can be found on Mark's website:

www.markhorrell.com/TheBaruntseAdventure

Made in the USA
Columbia, SC
13 June 2020